"In a world captivated and mesmerized by the cult of celebrity, this book helps us to reorient our hearts to experience the saints as ones that not only speak to our past but also shine the light and guide the path to our future. We stand on the shoulders of brothers and sisters in the faith who've faithfully shown us the way— and this resource helps make them accessible and relevant to our everyday lives. *Our Church Speaks* is a useful tool full of stunning artwork and meaningful prayers to help us to sit at the feet of saints young and old and learn from those who are a part of the great cloud of witnesses. For the past few years, I've been shaped and formed by these visuals online. I'm thrilled this collection has been published into a book we can now hold in our hands!"

J.R. Briggs, founder of Kairos Partnerships and author of *Fail* and *The Sacred Overlap*

"This isn't a history textbook but a lively introduction to a group of flawed but faith-filled followers of Christ spanning the breadth of the Christian church. You will come away from this book not just educated about these men and women but inspired to seek out the ways of the Spirit to which they point."

Russell Moore, editor in chief at *Christianity Today* and host of *The Russell Moore Show*

"Whenever I've encountered these arresting modern 'icons' on social media, I've always stopped scrolling in order to read further. To have them wonderfully collected into one winsome book is a gift to the church, especially as we seek to know and honor the global story of our great 'cloud of witnesses.'"

Jennifer L. Holberg, co-director of the Calvin Center for Faith and Writing at Calvin University and author of *Nourishing Narratives: The Power of Story to Shape Our Faith*

"Ben Lansing and D. J. Marotta invite readers to pull up a 'third chair' and join this dynamic duo 'at the table' for a transformative conversation. The table is set with a smorgasbord of spiritual delicacies that whet your appetite to know more about the Divine. They entice you with appetizers such as the Calendar of Saints and various theologians through the ages. Their 'dessert' is offered at the beginning, 'How To Use This Book As A Prayer Tool.' Such dessert enhances spiritual disciplines. This book made me feel that I could 'sup on this spiritual smorgasbord' while drawing closer to Yahweh!"

Barbara L. Peacock, author of *Soul Care in African American Practice* and founder of Peacock Soul Care

"The saints are not finally dead but are our living friends and mentors, alive with us in Christ now. We need their witness and their voice now. Which is why we need this beautiful book, especially with its ultimate aim of leading us into prayer— which is (as every saint insists) our truest work."

Winn Collier, director of the Eugene Peterson Center for Christian Imagination and author of *A Burning in My Bones: The Biography of Eugene Peterson*

"With so many reasons today to feel discouraged about the state of the Christian witness in the public square, Lansing and Marotta draw our attention to a cloud of witnesses—of saints and sinners, priests and poets, Asian and African, Byzantine and Baptist—who persevered in their devotion to Christ in the face of manifold temptations to become a faithless, hopeless, loveless people. This is a wonderful book for those who need a little encouragement to remain faithful, hopeful, and love-full in the face of their own temptations to become otherwise."

W. David O. Taylor, associate professor of theology and culture at Fuller Theological Seminary in Pasadena, California, and author of *Prayers for the Pilgrimage*

"I love *Our Church Speaks*! Ben Lansing and Dan Marotta are doing such a service to the church in our day by introducing us to so many saints, martyrs, and heroes from around the world. Each of them bore witness to the living Jesus with their lives—and with *Our Church Speaks*, Ben and Dan are doing the same. Check this book out! You'll be encouraged and inspired."

Caleb Maskell, professor of religion at Princeton University and associate national director of theology and education at Vineyard USA

"Like brilliant stained glass in cathedral windows, saints are people who let the light shine through: humans broken yet radiant and splendid, illuminated not by their own goodness but by God's glory. *Our Church Speaks* holds up preachers, healers, artists, reformers, women, men, and children, fifty-two saints from across times and places who scatter light of every imaginable hue. They inspire me with wonder: What are my own peculiar colors, created to display God's presence in the world?"

Karen Wright Marsh, author of *Vintage Saints and Sinners* and director of Theological Horizons

"I'm always grateful to see books that bring the rich history of the church to Christians today who need to hear such stories. I've followed *Our Church Speaks* on Instagram for a long time, and it's a delight to now have a sampling of their art and wisdom in this physical book—perfect for reading, savoring, praying over, and giving to friends and relatives as a gift."

Jennifer Woodruff Tait, senior editor of *Christian History* and author of *Christian History in Seven Sentences*

"This is a beautiful book. Reading it is like coming home to a family you forgot you had."

Justin Whitmel Earley, business lawyer and bestselling author of *The Common Rule*, *Habits of the Household*, and *Made for People*

BEN LANSING AND
D. J. MAROTTA

OUR
CHURCH
SPEAKS

AN ILLUSTRATED
DEVOTIONAL OF
SAINTS FROM EVERY
ERA AND PLACE

ivp

An imprint of InterVarsity Press
Downers Grove, Illinois

InterVarsity Press
P.O. Box 1400 | Downers Grove, IL 60515-1426
ivpress.com | email@ivpress.com

InterVarsity Press® is the publishing division of InterVarsity Christian Fellowship/USA®. For more information, visit www.intervarsity.org.

Scripture quotations, unless otherwise noted, are from The Holy Bible, English Standard Version, copyright © 2001 by Crossway Bibles, a division of Good News Publishers. Used by permission. All rights reserved.

Prayers and collects used and adapted from the *Book of Common Prayer, 1662 International Edition* with permission from InterVarsity Press.

Collects are taken from the Book of Common Prayer (2019).

Prayers adapted from the Book of Common Prayer (2019) are noted in the citations.

The Book of Common Prayer is copyright The Anglican Church in North America. Used with permission. All rights reserved.

Interior and cover Saints artwork is copyright Benjamin Terry Lansing.

Published in association with literary agent Don Gates of The Gates Group, www.the-gates-group.com.

While any stories in this book are true, some names and identifying information may have been changed to protect the privacy of individuals.

The publisher cannot verify the accuracy or functionality of website URLs used in this book beyond the date of publication.

Cover design: David Fassett
Interior design: Jeanna Wiggins
Images: © katatonia82 / iStock / Getty Images

ISBN 978-1-5140-0903-1 (print) | ISBN 978-1-5140-0905-5 (digital)

Printed in the United States of America ∞

Library of Congress Cataloging-in-Publication Data
A catalog record for this book is available from the Library of Congress.

30 29 28 27 26 25 24 | 12 11 10 9 8 7 6 5 4 3 2 1

■

To the people of Redeemer Anglican Church

in Richmond, Virginia;

especially our wives, Bethany and Rachel,

and the Marotta kids: June, Selah Rose, Wills, and John.

■

From earth's wide bounds, from ocean's farthest coast,

Through gates of pearl streams in the countless host,

Singing to Father, Son, and Holy Ghost,

Alleluia, Alleluia!

For All the Saints

CONTENTS

PREFACE

IN THE FALL OF 2016, the Lansings sat on a couch in the Marottas' living room to talk about a new church that was beginning in the heart of the city of Richmond, Virginia. Questions were asked, fears were shared, and prayers were prayed. By the end of the night, both couples sensed with confidence that we would share in the work of church planting together. And so we have. Over the years, the church has grown, and what began with apprehension has blossomed into true collaboration, friendship, and kingdom fruitfulness.

We share this because we want our readers to know that this book was born out of the colaboring we have shared in church together. Ben's work as a deacon and his love for art, history, and liturgy fueled his creation of the artwork, historical narrative, and the selection of the prayers in this book. Dan's experience as a priest, counselor, and church planter informed his pastoral insights as he wrote this book's devotional reflections. This book represents much of how we have walked with each other, sought to minister the gospel in our city, and helped each other grow in Christ over the years.

So think of reading this book as pulling up a third chair and joining the two of us at the table for a conversation. Welcome!

SAINTS OVER CELEBRITIES

WE LIVE IN THE AGE OF THE CELEBRITY.

Not that there haven't always been famous men and women. Every age has its jealousy-inducing fashionistas, heroes, and royalty. Success plus wealth plus stunning good looks is a winning formula no matter where or *when* you live. But the uniqueness of our time is found both in the sheer number of celebrities (thank you, internet) and in the desire of nearly every young person to become a celebrity (again, thank you, internet). Study after wearying study reports that the number one goal of most people under the age of thirty is not to cure cancer, or revitalize their hometown, or marry their high school sweetheart, but rather to be famous—to be a celebrity, to be recognized and praised for doing something rather than simply to do the thing.

This shift does two abominable things to the human soul:

1. It transforms virtue into vanity with such subtlety that the doer does not realize the target has moved.

2. It generates anxiety ex nihilo.

Now the doer must fret and fluster their way through the day trying to seduce their neighbor into worshiping them and feel no small amount of stress when outperformed by thousands of someones they have never met.

We are indeed stressed-out demigods.

The tonic for our vanity ulcers is not purchasing the latest habit-tracking daily planner (though I do love a good planner), embarking on a kale-only diet (is that even possible?), or chucking your smartphone into the Atlantic (tempting). Rather, we need to tune the frequency of our souls to the still-broadcasting song of the gospel being sung by the lives of men and women throughout the history of the church.

> Therefore, since we are surrounded by so great a cloud of witnesses, let us also lay aside every weight, and sin which clings so closely, and let us run with endurance the race that is set before us, looking to Jesus, the founder and perfecter of our faith, who for the joy that was set before him endured the cross, despising the shame, and is seated at the right hand of the throne of God. (Hebrews 12:1-2)

Saint Valentine, Saint Patrick, and Santa Claus—for many modern Christians, these may be the only recognizable names outside of Bible characters from two thousand years of church history. We know these names because of the civil calendar, though the memory of these saints has been secularized into consumerist oblivion.

Some of us may be well versed with Scripture but largely unacquainted with any Christians from the two millennia that separate us from the time of the apostles. Most of us are likely unaware of an ancient tool that Christians have used to rehearse this long history as a part of their daily lives, a tool called the *Calendar of Saints*.

THE CALENDAR OF SAINTS

Two thousand years ago, Christians were often hunted down and killed. Amid this darkness, the church began a radical practice. When a brother or sister was martyred for faith in Jesus, the Christian community remembered their date of death as an occasion for celebration and thanksgiving to God. This was a new birthday, when the beloved's body entered the grave in anticipation of resurrection and victory in Christ. The saints were not cherished for inherent moral perfection or superhuman niceness. They were broken and flawed, just like anyone. But their memory was preserved because, in their struggle with the world, the flesh, and the devil, the glory of Christ was particularly evident.

After many centuries, the calendar was filled with thousands of commemorations of martyrs and other faithful Christians and became known as the Calendar of Saints. The Christian liturgical calendar—with its seasons of Advent, Christmas, Epiphany, Lent, Easter, and Ordinary Time—and the Calendar of Saints functioned as complementary, daily rehearsals of the life of Christ and Christ's bride, the church. These rehearsals grounded the believer in what it meant to be in Christ as a part of his people.

By the Reformation of the sixteenth century, many Christians were concerned that celebrating saints had become a distraction from God's glory. This concern was not without reason; some people became so enamored of the cloud of witnesses that they forgot that the cloud should point the believer to Jesus, "the founder and perfecter of our faith" (Hebrews 12:2). Many Protestants abandoned the Calendar of Saints, and their church traditions lost a critical tool in rehearsing their history as part of the daily rhythms of life. The memory was lost. Today, many Christians feel rootless and deconstructed. We would benefit from reintroducing the Calendar of Saints, rightly contextualized around Christ.

The Calendar of Saints from which we draw in this book is populated by the broad scope of trinitarian Christianity, with representatives from various denominations and traditions. All are portrayed as members in the body of Christ, unified in his love and grace.

UNITY AMID DIVISION

In this divided world, it's tempting to be skeptical of this assumed unity. We can't ignore all of the conflicts between Christian denominations. Does presenting the saints of various traditions together give a false view of unity within the church?

In an essay titled "On the Reading of Old Books," C. S. Lewis (Anglican author of *Mere Christianity*) addressed this question. He mentioned the writings of many saints who had inspired him, including the ancient church father Augustine, the medieval theologian Thomas Aquinas, the Puritan John Bunyan, the Anglican reformer Richard Hooker, and the Roman Catholic counterreformer Francis de Sales. Lewis commented:

> They are, you will note, a mixed bag, representative of many Churches, climates and ages. . . . The divisions of Christendom are undeniable and are by some of these writers most fiercely expressed. But if any man is tempted to think . . . that "Christianity" is a word of so many

meanings that it means nothing at all, he can learn beyond all doubt, by stepping out of his own century, that this is not so. Measured against the ages, "mere Christianity" turns out to be no insipid inter-denominational transparency, but something positive, self-consistent, and inexhaustible.... We are all rightly distressed, and ashamed also, at the divisions of Christendom. But those who have always lived within the Christian fold may be too easily dispirited by them. They are bad, but such people do not know what it looks like from without. Seen from there, what is left intact despite all the divisions, still appears (as it truly is) an immensely formidable unity.[1]

Lewis's message is convicting. Denominational divisions are undeniable and often exist for real and substantive reasons. It would be a mistake to assume that achieving perfect unity in the church is any easier than achieving harmony in the deep divisions of any other family. Yet for those who spend time grappling with important theological nuances, Lewis reminds us that the church, in all its traditions, continues to hold a profound unity that has remained constant throughout the centuries and traditions.

MEETING OUR FAMILY

This vision of the church inspires the art in this book. Here is the church in raw honesty, with all its conflicts, divisions, and family squabbles. And yet, holistically, it is still a family of *immense, formidable unity* in Christ Jesus.

The art series *Our Church Speaks* and the selection presented in this book can help restore the memory of these saints and the words they have passed down to us. In this art series, we see the broad scope of the family of Christ. The online *Our Church Speaks* consists of over 250 portraits, with more on the way. Fifty-two of these portraits were chosen for this book, one saint or group of saints for each week of the year. Others can be viewed at www.ourchurchspeaks.com.

This book's "cloud of witnesses" are deacons, priests, and bishops. They are artists, poets, and musicians. Rulers and enslaved. Men and women. Monks and parents. Children and elderly. They are converts from various world religions. They are Baptists, Roman Catholics, Anglicans, Presbyterians, Lutherans, Eastern Orthodox, and Methodists. They are from every inhabited continent and all twenty centuries of the church's history. If you are a baptized Christian, this is the family of Christ you are reborn into. This is our church, and it continues to speak today. May the lives and words of these saints inspire us, challenge us, and urge us on as we "run with endurance the race that is set before us, looking to Jesus" (Hebrews 12:1-2).

It is said that those who do not know history are doomed to repeat it. Oh, if only that were true! Then we might accidentally become another Harriet Tubman or Augustine of Hippo without doing anything! Let it rather be said that those who do not know history are doomed to wallow in the worst parts. History is not all futility and tragedy. There are lighthouses built along the rocky shoals, and the attentive voyager may navigate treacherous waters by them.

The saints of the church flicker like candles along a dark corridor. They are not 1400-watt LED floodlights to blind you with their brilliance; those are the celebrities. A celebrity is a flashbulb straight to the cornea.

The celebrity demands, "Look at me!"

The saint whispers, "Look to God."

The celebrity says, "Try to be like me, but you'll never be like me."

The saint says, "Why would anyone want to be like me? Who has God made *you*?"

The celebrity is ever ascending, climbing the tower of Babel to the double-platinum throne.

The saint is ever descending, saying, "Please have my seat, I insist."

The celebrity offers you everything you want but can never have.

The saint offers you the thing you fear but will redeem your soul.

The celebrity is a Ferrari screaming down the highway with music blaring.

The saint is the freshwater creek beside the highway that almost nobody ever notices and is nearly impossible to hear over the roar of traffic.

Yet the water murmurs as it wanders over stones and around oak roots. It is not silent.

Our church speaks. Those who have ears, let them hear.

HOW TO USE THIS BOOK AS A PRAYER TOOL

The historic church has regularly commemorated the saints with thanksgiving and praise to God for their life and witness. You can continue this tradition with this short liturgy.

Turn to any saint's entry in this book. You may want to select an entry with a commemoration day closest to your current date. Then begin:

Opening Prayer (based on Psalm 51:15): O Lord, open my lips, and my mouth will declare your praise. Glory be to the Father, and the Son, and the Holy Spirit. As it was in the beginning, is now, and ever shall be, forever and ever. Amen.

Scripture Reading: Read aloud the passage of Scripture associated with the saint of the week. Consider exploring the broader context of this passage by reading the entire chapter in your Bible.

Reflection: Take time for a period of silence and stillness. Consider the following reflection points about the entry. (You may want to take only one reflection point per day, giving yourself a full week of prayer and reflection.)

- Read the saint's quotation and contemplate its meaning. Are there implications that speak to your life circumstances?
- Study the details of the artwork. What stands out to you?
- Read the saint's biography. What do you find convicting, challenging, or inspiring about their story?
- Consider how the Scripture reading speaks to the life and work of the saint.
- Read the associated devotional reflection.
- Ask the Holy Spirit how he may be leading you, considering what you have read.
- Pray the entry's accompanying prayer of thanksgiving for God's power, manifested in his saints.

The Lord's Prayer: Our Father, who art in heaven, hallowed be thy name. Thy kingdom come. Thy will be done on earth as it is in heaven. Give us this day our daily bread, and forgive us our trespasses, as we forgive those who trespass against us. Lead us not into temptation, but deliver us from evil. For thine is the kingdom and the power and the glory, forever and ever. Amen.

Closing Sentence: Glory to God, whose power working in us can do infinitely more than we can ask or imagine. Glory to him from generation to generation in the church, and in Christ Jesus forever and ever. Amen (based on Ephesians 3:20-21).[2]

BISHOP OF CONSTANTINOPLE AND
TEACHER OF THE FAITH *(c. 329–390)*

Commemoration: January 2
Time: Fourth century
Place: Cappadocia (now Turkey)

> *As a fish cannot swim without water, and as a bird cannot fly without air, so a Christian cannot advance a single step without Christ.*[1]

At a pivotal time in church history, God called an aspiring poet named Gregory to "contend for the faith that was once for all delivered to the saints" (Jude 1:3). Though ministry was not Gregory's first chosen vocation, God used him mightily to minister to the church and equipped him with good friends who stood by his side in his important calling.

Gregory of Nazianzus was the son of Greek landowners in Cappadocia (now central Turkey). His mother had been a Christian for many years. His father converted to Christianity a short time before Gregory's birth and served the church as the bishop of Nazianzus.[2] Young Gregory had no interest in the burdens of life as a clergyman and instead wished to become a poet and scholar. But his perspective began to change while journeying to Athens to study rhetoric. His ship hit a furious storm, and all aboard feared their end had come. In this moment of desperation, Gregory dedicated his life to Jesus Christ. The ship was spared, and Gregory arrived safely in Athens.

In Athens, Gregory studied alongside Basil and Julian, who would come to play significant roles in Gregory's life:[3] Basil became Gregory's lifelong best friend; Julian, a nephew of Emperor Constantine the Great, would become one of Gregory's greatest foes.

After several years of study, Gregory and Basil were urged by their families to redirect their career ambitions. Gregory's father appealed to him to assist with the needs of the church of Nazianzus. Basil, who had hoped to become a celebrated lawyer, was encouraged by his sister, Macrina, to devote himself to prayer and ministry.

Able and faithful ministers were certainly needed, as the church faced challenges without and within. Gregory's old schoolmate, Julian, became emperor and renounced Christianity, vowing to uproot the faith and replace it with Roman paganism. Meanwhile, a significant dispute spread within the church about the nature of Jesus. Who really was Jesus? Was he created or was he the eternal Creator of all things? The Council of Nicaea had attempted to settle this dispute many decades earlier by drafting a creed of scriptural answers to this question. The Nicene Creed affirmed that Jesus was "of the same substance" as God the Father and one of three persons within the Trinity. But many in church leadership later compromised the faith and undermined Nicaea's teachings. For a time, it seemed only one elderly bishop, Athanasius, was left to defend the Council of Nicaea's theological language.

Gregory and Basil initially resisted the call to make a stand during this critical moment. But in time, they acknowledged that the Lord was indeed calling them to redirect their ambitions. Gregory, Basil, and Basil's siblings fully devoted themselves to defending the ancient apostolic faith, as summarized by the Nicene Creed. This band of friends became bishops, theologians, and monastic leaders known today as the Cappadocians. Through dedicated prayer and service, they preserved and advanced the Christian faith.[4]

Gregory was noted for his beautiful writings and sermons and revered for his just leadership. As an old man, he was made bishop of Constantinople, then the largest city on earth. A new church council met in Constantinople to affirm the teachings of Nicaea. Gregory's theological clarifications about the Holy Spirit became part of the council's expanded version of the Nicene Creed. And Gregory never abandoned his love of poetry, despite his career shift toward ministry. His theological and autobiographical poems became powerful and enduring expressions of trinitarian faith.

SCRIPTURE

"Jesus said to them, 'Truly, truly I say to you, before Abraham was, I am.'" (John 8:58)

MEDITATION: THE KING HAS BECOME YOUR FRIEND

The old heresies never really die; they evolve. Arianism is an ancient heresy that defines Jesus as a divine creation and certainly not coequal with God the Father. While most people in the world are Arians, what's interesting is that today many self-proclaiming Christians are private Arians as well. This may be true of you even if you've never heard of Arianism or of Gregory of Nazianzus's labors against it.

Private Arianism shows up in an overly cozy, chummy relationship with Jesus that is not counterbalanced with fear, awe, respect, submission, and worship. Private Arianism looks like Jesus as: buddy, therapist, life coach, helper, prayer answerer, spouse finder, raise getter.

Point of clarity: of course, Christ can accomplish all these little things and more, but the problem with this kind of friendship with Jesus is that it just isn't worth very much. Jesus is one friend among many. It's not bad, but it's not great either. It's like frozen yogurt. It's just . . . okay.

The upside of orthodoxy (theological orthodoxy is actually full of up-sides) is that if you behold Jesus as capital G-O-D and recognize the car-penter from Nazareth as the creator, sustainer, and ultimate judge of all things, then you must, *must* fall down before him in complete and utter submission.

If you reach this point, you will experience the most wonderfully sur-prising of privileges: the King shall stretch forth his hand and raise you up and embrace you.

You see, in Jesus, the King has become your friend. This kind of friendship is vastly more weighty, substantive, and valuable than the first kind.

The cozy counselor/friend? Not worth much. The Lord of the universe calls you friend? Worth everything.

PRAYER

Almighty God, you gave your servant Gregory of Nazianzus special gifts of grace to understand and teach the truth revealed in Christ Jesus. Grant that by this teaching we may know you, the one true God, and Jesus Christ whom you have sent, who lives and reigns with you and the Holy Spirit, one God, forever and ever. Amen.[5]

MISSIONARY *(1848–1915)*

Commemoration: January 11
Time: Nineteenth and twentieth centuries
Place: Scotland and Nigeria

Lord, the task is impossible for me, but not for thee.
Lead the way and I will follow.[1]

MANY NIGERIANS REVERE MARY SLESSOR as a messenger of mercy who transformed society through the gospel of hope. She grew up in a working-class Presbyterian family in Scotland. Stories of Christian missionaries in Africa like David Livingstone inspired Slessor. Family hardship forced Slessor to work in a factory as a child, but she resolved to become a missionary, no matter the obstacles. While working in a mill in Dundee, she studied African languages in her spare minutes at work, during walks to and from home, and in the late-night hours.

After years of study, Slessor got a teaching position in Calabar, Nigeria, in 1875. The Calabar coast had long been a center of the transatlantic slave trade and had a reputation as one of the deadliest regions on earth. Though the trade had been officially outlawed decades before Slessor's arrival, the trauma of slavery left deep scars in the Calabar cultural memory. Slessor soon realized that her work in Nigeria would extend far beyond her teaching position. She ministered to those suffering from smallpox and developed economic opportunities to give women greater security and autonomy. Local superstition considered twins the offspring of evil spirits, so the babies were abandoned in clay pots and the mother was often put to death. Slessor adopted abandoned children whenever she found them and preached the good news that Jesus Christ had forever defeated the world of evil spirits and that a good and loving God had reconciled the world to himself.

Slessor gained respect among the locals for her humility, proficiency in local languages and customs, and ability to help resolve disputes among conflicting tribes. She settled among the Okoyong people, and her home became known as an outpost of compassion, healing, and the light of Christ.

SCRIPTURE

"Behold, children are a heritage from the LORD, the fruit of the womb a reward." (Psalm 127:3)

MEDITATION: DEFENDER OF CHILDREN

Pharaoh viewed the Hebrews as a growing threat to the Egyptian way of life, so he ordered all Hebrew baby boys killed. King Herod feared that a future king would arise from Bethlehem, so he ordered all boys ages two and under to be killed in that region.

In first-century Rome, it was common practice to leave unwanted children, especially baby girls, to die of exposure to the elements. Child sacrifice was common in the Incan Empire. Three thousand bones of sacrificed young children have been excavated on Sardinia in the Mediterranean. In China, there is a long tradition of valuing male children over female children. As the philosopher Han Fei Tzu wrote, "A father and mother, when they produce a boy, congratulate each other; but when they produce a girl, they put her to death."[2] In Japan, the practice of *mabiki*, which literally means to pull plants from an overcrowded garden, was used as a form of population control. Parents would often suffocate their second or third sons. Daughters were usually spared because they could be married off or sold as servants or prostitutes.

On every continent, in nearly every culture, in every age, there is a tragic history of the devaluing and killing of children. In our own age, abortions and child abandonment continue this pattern.

This is one of the most important ways in which the Christian faith offers cultural critique and seeks the common good for every society it encounters. When the church enters a culture for the very first time, one of the first things that often happens is immediate advocacy and intervention on behalf of children. This is the story and legacy of Mary Slessor, and she stands in a long, diverse, beautiful tradition of elevating children to a place of equal value and status in the eyes of adults.

Followers of Jesus do this not only because our Lord said, "Let the little children come to me and do not hinder them" (Matthew 19:14), but also because in the incarnation of the Son of God, the second person of the Holy Trinity became a human baby. The birth of Christ, the Word made flesh, dignifies all children everywhere.

PRAYER

O God, you desire that all people be saved and come to knowledge of the truth. Just as you prospered the ministry of Mary Slessor in Nigeria, so prosper all those who live, preach, and teach the gospel at home and in distant lands; protect them in all perils, support them in their loneliness, sustain them in the hour of trial, give them your abundant grace to bear faithful witness, and endue them with burning zeal and love, that they may turn many to righteousness through Jesus Christ our Lord. Amen.[3]

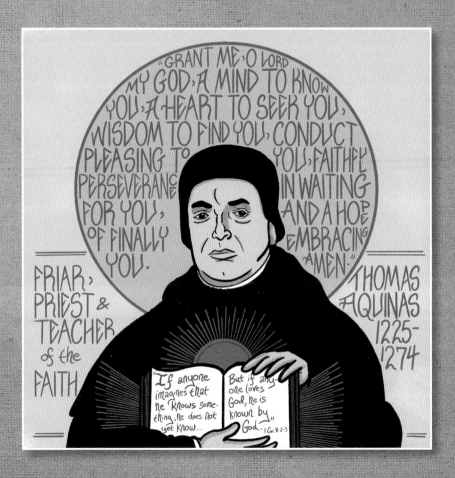

FRIAR, PRIEST, AND TEACHER OF THE FAITH *(1225–1274)*

Commemoration: January 28
Time: Thirteenth century
Place: Kingdom of Sicily (now Italy)

Grant me, O Lord my God, a mind to know you, a heart to seek you,
wisdom to find you, conduct pleasing to you, faithful perseverance
in waiting for you, and a hope of finally embracing you. Amen.[1]

OF THE MEDIEVAL CHURCH'S MANY INTELLECTUAL LEADERS, none has had more influence than the philosophical theologian Thomas Aquinas. He was born to a noble family near Naples, Italy, and joined the Dominican Order of Preachers as a teenager. At the time, the Dominicans were a new monastic movement that lacked prestige and social standing. The Dominicans required their members to renounce personal wealth as part of their mission to renew sound doctrine and holy life within the church. Thomas's family was appalled that their son would join such a radical group and locked him in their castle tower, hoping to dissuade him with rich foods and comforts. Thomas would not succumb and made the most of his time. He tutored his sisters, prayed, memorized Scripture, and read deeply. After two years of imprisonment, his family finally relented, and Thomas was released to study with the Dominicans.

At school, Thomas was nicknamed "the Dumb Ox" because of his heavy stature, shy disposition, and slowness of speech. One of Thomas's teachers, recognizing his talents, told his class, "I assure you the bellowing of that ox will one day fill the world."[2] In time, the wisdom of this "Dumb Ox" became evident to all, and his nickname changed to "the Angelic Doctor."

Thomas was equipped with a deep understanding of Scripture, early church writings, classical Greek philosophy, and Jewish and Islamic thought. But beyond intellect, Thomas was renewed daily by his love for Jesus Christ, and this love fueled his work. Thomas's writings plumbed the depths of God's mysteries as far as human language, reason, and intellect could take him. His greatest writing, the *Summa Theologica* (*Summary of Theology*), summarizes the beliefs of the Western medieval church. It explored the Catholic theology of God, creation, humanity, law, grace, existence, and the sacraments. Yet Thomas left the *Summa* unfinished. While at Mass several months before his death, Thomas received a vision of God so profound that it transcended human comprehension and expression. The vision left him so awestruck that he set down his writing pen forever. Thomas said, "Everything [I have written] seems to me straw—compared with the vision I have had."[3] In saying this, Thomas upheld the truth of his earlier writings but recognized the limits of understanding in this life.

In his final days, Thomas found inspiration in the rapturous love of God expressed in the Song of Solomon. On his deathbed, he lifted his eyes to heaven and said, "Come, my beloved, let us head out to the garden."⁴ He died at age forty-eight, entering the eternal garden where his intellectual pursuit and awe-filled love of God would have no end.

SCRIPTURE

"What no eye has seen, nor ear heard, nor the heart of man imagined, what God has prepared for those who love him." (1 Corinthians 2:9)

MEDIATION: SEEKING THE MYSTERY

"I'm tired of trying to nail down every loose theological board," said the older and much wiser pastor sitting across the table in the diner. The man was no intellectual slouch: Harvard undergrad; Westminster seminary; books published; leader of large, important churches; chancellor of a seminary . . . and yet he had reached the limit of his ability to wrap his homo-sapien brain around God.

Thomas Aquinas reached the same terminus, as has every serious student of Scripture and biblical, philosophical theology. At some point (depending on one's cognitive capacities), you hit the wall. Or rather, you reach the end of the trail, and before you lies the Grand Canyon of mystery.

The problem for most of us is that, since we know the trail ends, we think the hike is not worth the trouble. We sequester the intellectual pursuit of God on to back shelves with labels like "dry," "emotionless," "pharisaical," and "head knowledge" (as if there were any other kind). From the comfort of our living room sofas, we congratulate ourselves on being more spiritual, more *Christian* than those neutered, tweed-sporting, library gnomes with their Greek and Hebrew lexicons and their Aristotle and their interpretive theories. Don't they know that the things of God are a mystery? We know better. We can more fully appreciate the Grand Canyon from our armchairs.

Thomas's life and legacy speaks against such arrogant slothfulness. Lace up your boots, man! The mysteries of God are not delivered by Amazon to your doorstep; they lie hundreds of miles down the trail—over mountain ranges, beyond swamps, past packs of wolves, and yes, even through books and professors.

To the theology snob, Thomas speaks a seasoned word of caution: the synapses in your brain will fall short; you cannot nail down every loose theological board.

To the antitheology snob, Thomas speaks a rousing word of motivation: get going! It is often those who stretch their gray matter to the breaking point who reap the rewards of experiencing the wonder of divine mystery.

A PRAYER OF THOMAS AQUINAS

Give me, O Lord, a steadfast heart, which no unworthy thought can drag down; an unconquered heart, which no tribulation can wear out; an upright heart, which no unworthy purpose can tempt aside. Bestow upon me understanding to know you, diligence to seek you, wisdom to find you, and faithfulness that finally may embrace you. Amen.[5]

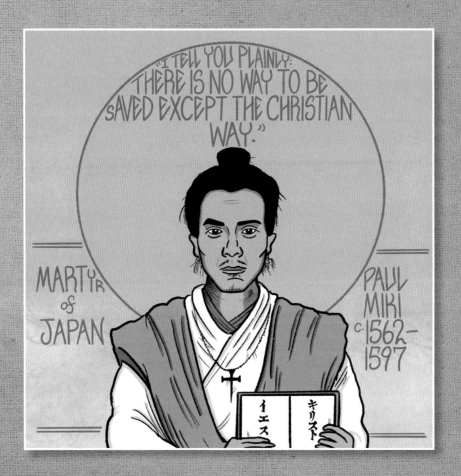

MARTYR OF JAPAN *(c. 1562–1597)*

Commemoration: February 6
Time: Sixteenth century
Place: Japan

I tell you plainly: there is no way to be saved except the Christian way.[1]

CHRISTIANITY FIRST REACHED JAPAN IN 1549, due to the heroic missionary work of the Jesuit priest Francis Xavier and his companions. In the next sixty years, over three hundred thousand Japanese citizens converted to Christianity.[2] Conversions became so widespread that the Japanese ruling class suspected Christians were seeking to overthrow the government and colonize and enslave the Japanese people. The ruler, Hideyoshi, issued an order for the arrest and execution of Christians. Japanese evangelist Paul Miki was on track to become the first Japanese-born Christian priest, but he was arrested before this aspiration was fulfilled. He was among a group of twenty-six Christians who were rounded up and forced to undergo a six-hundred-mile march from Kyoto to their place of execution in Nagasaki. As they walked, Miki tried to convert those they encountered, and the prisoners sang an ancient Christian hymn, the *Te Deum*: "We praise you, O God; we proclaim you as Lord. All the earth worships you, the Father everlasting." When they reached their destination, they were crucified. Paul Miki delivered his final sermon from his cross: "After Christ's example, I forgive my persecutors. I do not hate them. I ask God to have pity on all, and I hope that my blood will fall on my fellow men as fruitful rain."[3]

Christianity was suppressed in Japan for the next two and a half centuries. Missionaries were expelled from Japan, thousands of Christians were crucified or burned at the stake, and many Christians were ordered to trample on images of Christ or suffer martyrdom. Seven generations of underground Christians persisted in secret until 1871, when the Japanese government finally gave them legal protection. Nagasaki, where Miki and his companions suffered martyrdom, became the center of Japanese Christianity and today is home to the largest population of Christians in Japan.

SCRIPTURE

"But I say to you who hear, Love your enemies, do good to those who
hate you, bless those who curse you, pray for those who abuse you."
(Luke 6:27-28)

MEDITATION: WHEN YOUR NEIGHBOR IS YOUR ENEMY

Jesus taught his followers to love two groups of people: neighbors and enemies. While we have no record of him explicitly teaching that these two kinds of people might sometimes be the same person, he certainly experienced it. Jesus was not betrayed, accused, mocked, scourged, and sent to be crucified by faceless, nameless agents of the state, but rather by friends, neighbors, coworkers, and fellow citizens. Jesus' suffering was personal—emotional and relational, just as much as it was physical.

And that's all just at the human level. At the divine level, Jesus suffered under the hands of his own creation, hands he had *made*. Jesus was betrayed with words from mouths and lungs filled with air that he created.

Often the enemies we hate the most are neighbors who have wounded us. We may feel general contempt for political leaders or pundits that we see online, but our deepest animosity is always directed toward people who have hurt us personally. Real enemies have names, faces, and addresses. Sometimes the most bitter enemy is someone you used to love. Maybe someone you used to think loved you.

And yet Jesus' love persisted, and he loved his neighbor enemies all the way to the end.

This is the Christian faith's bewildering neighbor love and enemy love. It is love toward those who are unsafe.

Paul Miki sought to embody this kind of love toward his neighbors who became his enemies. Likely the people who marched him six hundred miles to Nagasaki and crucified him there were not faceless, nameless agents of the state, but former friends. They were likely neighbors.

As Christ's blood became the life-source of the church, so Miki's blood fell from his broken body into the ground in Nagasaki and, over the centuries, slowly fertilized the soil until it began to produce abundant fruit in a growing church. Nagasaki was transformed from a Japanese Golgotha to a foretaste of the new Jerusalem.

This is what it looks like when the kingdom of heaven encounters the kingdom of this world. It's a bloodbath. But from the blood is born a new humanity that practices the way of peace.

How tragic that, years later, those neighbors in Nagasaki were destroyed by an atomic bomb dropped by baptized American Christians because Japan was their enemy. Upon the fortieth anniversary of the bombing of Hiroshima and Nagasaki, these words were spoken by Father George Zabelka, the US Air Force chaplain who served as a priest for the airmen who dropped the atomic bombs:

> The bombing of Nagasaki means even more to me than the bombing of Hiroshima. By August 9, 1945, we knew what that bomb would do, but we still dropped it. We knew that agonies and sufferings would ensue, and we also knew—at least our leaders knew—that it was not necessary. The Japanese were already defeated. They were already suing for peace. But we insisted on unconditional surrender. . . . As a Catholic chaplain I watched as the Boxcar, piloted by a good Irish Catholic pilot, dropped the bomb on Urakami Cathedral in Nagasaki, the center of Catholicism in Japan. I knew that St. Francis Xavier, centuries before, had brought the Catholic faith to Japan. I knew that schools, churches, and religious orders were annihilated. And yet I said nothing.[4]

The tragic irony of the destruction of Nagasaki should not be forgotten; rather it should serve as a constant, sobering reminder that the way of Jesus looks more like Paul Miki and less like an atomic bomb.

A PRAYER OF FRANCIS XAVIER, MISSIONARY TO JAPAN

O God, grant that we may desire you, and desiring you seek you, and seeking you find you, and finding you be satisfied in you forever. Amen.[5]

MONASTIC AND PROPHETIC WITNESS *(c. 1869–1947)*

Commemoration: February 8
Time: Nineteenth and twentieth centuries
Place: Darfur (Sudan) and Italy

I am definitively loved and whatever happens to me,
I am awaited by this love. And so my life is good.[1]

JOSEPHINE BAKHITA'S LIFE IS A TESTAMENT of God's faithfulness in the darkest circumstances. She was born in Darfur, Sudan, among the Daju people. Her first years were happy, but at age eight she was kidnapped by Arab slave traders. For twelve years, she was bought and sold multiple times, forced to convert to Islam, and subjected to cruel beatings and scarification. Bakhita later recalled that a day did not go by when she did not receive a wound of some kind. Her body bore 114 scars from her time in slavery. The trauma caused her to forget her birth name, and she was ironically given the Arabic name Bakhita (meaning "fortunate").

Eventually, Bakhita was purchased by an Italian government agent and brought to Italy, where she served as a maid for an Italian family. While the family was traveling out of the country, Bakhita was sent to live with nuns in a monastic community in Venice. Bakhita recalled that "those holy mothers instructed me with heroic patience and introduced me to that God who from childhood I had felt in my heart without knowing who He was."[2] Bakhita refused to leave the convent, and her case was challenged legally. The courts ruled that her servitude was illegal and she was to be free. Her first decision as a free person was to join the monastic society that had introduced her to Jesus. After Bakhita was baptized, she served at a convent in Schio, northwest of Venice. During her forty-two years in Schio, she earned a reputation in her community for her gentle voice, profound faith, and life of prayer.

SCRIPTURE

"Blessed are the poor in spirit, for theirs is the kingdom of heaven." (Matthew 5:3)

MEDITATION: THE PARADOX OF POVERTY

The word that our English Bibles translate as *blessed* in the beatitudes of the Gospel of Matthew is the Greek word *makarioi*, which means something akin to happy, fortunate, enviable, or congratulatory. In this beatitude, Jesus is making a paradoxical statement about his new reality: it is those who are run down, worn out, beaten up, or ground to dust that will end up reigning in his kingdom.

This is illogical and offensive. Poverty of body or spirit is objectively bad and in nearly all cultures is understood as a sign of life poorly lived. Why would Jesus say that those who are not living well are blessed?

When you realize that you are weak, that you are poor, that you need the lowest, most base form of charity, that you don't have what it takes, that you aren't enough, that you're not going to make it, that you're dependent, that you need help—*then* the beatitude applies to you, and you are blessed because, in Jesus, God *does* help you.

Q: What do you contribute toward your salvation?

A: Your need and your openness to receiving help.

It's like the line in the old hymn "Come, Ye Sinners": "Let not conscience make you linger, / Nor of fitness fondly dream; / All the fitness He requires / Is to feel your need of Him."[3]

The gospel paradox of poverty is that, through the gospel, the most needy, dependent people end up with all the riches in the end. It's not the comfort of capitalism, where if you outcompete your neighbor, you get blessed. It's not the comfort of Marxism, where you overthrow your rich neighbor and take his stuff to get blessed. It's not the comfort of therapy, where you must learn coping mechanisms to deal with the poverty of your spirit in order to feel blessed. It's not the comfort of traditional religion, where you must overcome your spiritual poverty with willpower and discipline to be rewarded with God's blessing.

None of these can offer the poor and the poor in spirit what Jesus can offer.

In Jesus, God has become poor and poor in spirit, and he has done so to lift you up in resurrection and to give you the riches of his kingdom—as a free gift.

Young, enslaved Josephine Bakhita was the epitome of poor in spirit, and it was a cruel thing to nickname her "fortunate/lucky." However, in the gospel paradox of poverty, she knew the love and blessing of salvation through Jesus. She ended up keeping the name because, in Jesus, she really was fortunate after all.

PRAYER

O God, almighty and merciful, you healed the broken heart of your daughter Josephine Bakhita and turned her sorrow into joy: Let your fatherly goodness be upon all whom you have made. Remember in pity all those who are this day destitute and forgotten in slavery and human trafficking. Bless the multitude of your poor. Lift up and liberate the bodies and souls of those who are cast down. Mightily befriend innocent sufferers, and sanctify to them the endurance of their wrongs. Though they are perplexed, save them from despair. Grant this, O Lord, for the love of him who for our sakes became poor—your Son, our Savior, Jesus Christ. Amen.[4]

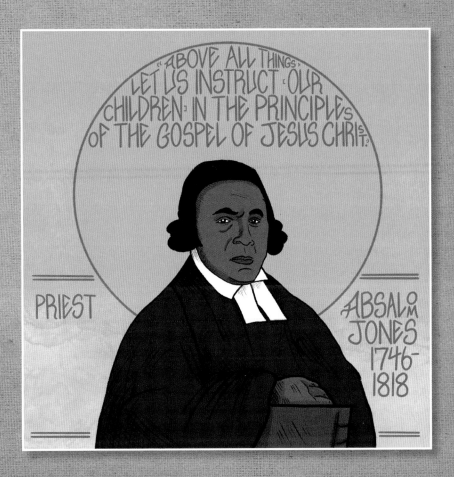

PRIEST *(1746–1818)*

Commemoration: February 13
Time: Eighteenth and nineteenth centuries
Place: Pennsylvania (United States)

Above all things, let us instruct [our children] in the principles of the gospel of Jesus Christ, whereby they may become wise unto salvation.[1]

SINCE BEFORE THE FOUNDING OF THE UNITED STATES, the African American church has been a prophetic voice in American culture. Absalom Jones was an eminent founding father of this Christian tradition. He was born enslaved in Delaware and, in his youth, witnessed his family sold away. As an adult, he purchased freedom for his wife and children and, eventually, for himself. Jones befriended Richard Allen, also a freed slave. The two became lay ministers at St. George Methodist Episcopal Church in Philadelphia, a church with both white and black congregants, where black ministers were allowed to preach. Together, they founded the Free African Society in 1787, an organization that championed the rights of free black citizens.

In the late eighteenth century, segregationists took control at St. George and forced African Americans to sit together in the balcony, separate from the white congregants. This change came abruptly. In the middle of a service, Jones was kneeling in prayer when he was approached by an usher and told to sit in the segregated section of the church. When Jones did not immediately comply, he was pulled to his feet by the usher, who was unwilling to wait until the prayer was over.[2] Jones and Allen led a historic church walkout in response to this mistreatment.

Soon after, the city of Philadelphia was hit by a devastating plague of yellow fever. Ten percent of the city died. Jones, Allen, and the members of the Free African Society courageously ministered to the sick and dying, including those segregationists who had oppressed them.

Jones rose to prominence as an influential Christian leader in the city of Philadelphia. He established the African Episcopal Church of St. Thomas, a church with a mission "to arise out of the dust and shake ourselves, and throw off that servile fear, that the habit of oppression and bondage trained us up in. And in meekness and fear, we would desire to walk in the liberty wherewith Christ has made us free."[3] Richard Allen, likewise, established the Bethel African Methodist Episcopal Church (known as Mother Bethel AME), the first independent black church in the Methodist tradition. St. Thomas and Bethel became two of the most significant congregations in Philadelphia, and Jones and Allen became two of the first officially ordained African American pastors of any church in the United States. Jones preached antislavery sermons every New Year's Day, a tradition he faithfully continued until his death in 1818.

SCRIPTURE

"Thus says the LORD, the God of Israel, 'Let my people go, that they may hold a feast to me in the wilderness.'" (Exodus 5:1)

MEDITATION: WHAT IS FREEDOM FOR?

There is a lot of talk about freedom these days. Most people use the word to mean unconstrained, unlimited, uninhibited, able to do as we please, to follow our desires, so long as they do not harm someone else. Within this construct, bondage is anything or anyone who keeps us from living the kind of life we would like to live, and freedom is simply the removal of the bonds of oppression. Exodus is the original liberation story, if there ever was one. All freedom fighters are riffing off Moses. What is interesting is that this original freedom story is not only concerned with freedom *from* bondage, but freedom *to* something entirely new and different.

"Let my people go" is a famous phrase, but the second half of that sentence "that they may hold a feast to me in the wilderness" is far less well known. God (not Moses) set his people free from slavery not so that they could do as they please, but so that they might celebrate his provision, even in the midst of desolation. After plagues, parting of the Red Sea, Mount Sinai, the golden calf, the Ten Commandments, and more, that is exactly what they did. The manna that fell from heaven became the feast of God's provision even in their forty years of wandering the wilderness.

This feast points forward to the new Moses, Jesus, who not only sets us free from enslavement to sin but also provides a new feast in the wilderness, the Lord's Supper, also called the Eucharist. This simple meal reminds us not only what we have been set free *from*, but what we have been set free *to*. Our freedom in Christ is purposeful—that we may worship him, be nurtured by him, and continually draw our life from him.

Absalom Jones not only knew this, but he lived it. He not only sought freedom from slavery for himself, but he used his freedom to serve as a pastor, administering the bread and wine of the Eucharist (the feast in the wilderness). What kind of person would use their freedom to serve in such a way? Only someone with the mind of Christ.

PRAYER

Our God, in whom we trust, who empowered your servant Absalom Jones to become a beacon amid the darkness of prejudice and fear, strengthen us not to regard overmuch who is for us or who is against us, but to see to it that we be with you in everything we do. Amen.[4]

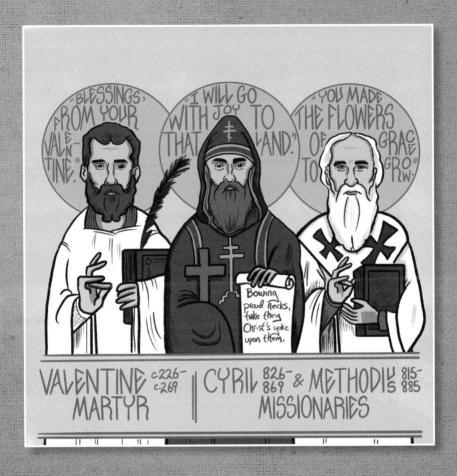

VALENTINE, MARTYR *(c. 226–c. 269)*
CYRIL, MISSIONARY *(826–869)*
METHODIUS, MISSIONARY *(815–885)*

Commemoration: February 14
Time: Third century (Valentine) and ninth century (Cyril and Methodius)
Place: Rome (Valentine) and Eastern Europe (Cyril and Methodius)

Blessings, from your Valentine. VALENTINE[1]
I will go with joy to that land. CYRIL[2]
You made the flowers of grace to grow. METHODIUS[3]

THOUGH THE ROMAN PRIEST VALENTINE and the Byzantine brothers Cyril and Methodius served the Lord in different centuries and different regions of the world, their commemorations fall on the same day. Saints are often remembered on the date of their death, and both Valentine and Cyril are believed to have died on February 14.

Valentine was a priest in Rome when Emperor Claudius II began his hostile reign. Valentine was arrested for performing Christian weddings. While imprisoned, Valentine befriended the jailer's daughter and healed her of blindness. Valentine was eventually sentenced to death and, on the morning of his execution, left a final note of encouragement and blessing to the little girl, signed, "From your Valentine." This note is said to have inspired the common greetings exchanged on Valentine's Day.

Six centuries after Valentine laid down his life for his friends and for Christ, the brothers Cyril and Methodius were inspired by this same Christian love to leave the comforts of the Byzantine Empire and journey into the dangerous lands of the pagan Slavs, preaching the good news of God's love. Their heroic missionary work involved developing a writing system for the Slavic language, allowing the Slavic people to translate and propagate God's Word in their own language. Cyrillic script (named after Cyril) is widely used in Eastern Europe to this day and was instrumental in making the Word of God available in Slavic lands, including Ukraine, Russia, Bulgaria, and Serbia.[4] Today, Cyril and Methodius are remembered as spiritual fathers to the Slavic peoples and founders of the modern Slavic languages.

SCRIPTURE

"For God so loved the world, that he gave his only Son, that whoever believes in him should not perish but have eternal life." (John 3:16)

MEDITATION: THE NATURE OF LOVE

Most people in the world fall into one of two camps: those who are infatuated with love and those who are totally disillusioned with love. The starry-eyed lovers feel they are swimming in a wavy ocean of love. Their beloveds—be they romantic boyfriends or girlfriends or spouses, faithful parents, delightful children, treasured grandparents, or any other relation—are the most important people in their lives. It's not all roses, but overall, love is the theme of their relationships, and relationships are the theme of their life. The disillusioned have been shipwrecked on the ocean of love and now know love can be a dangerous siren that sets you up only to tear you down. Love is dangerous, destructive. Love is an angler fish in the depths of the Mariana Trench. It holds out a tantalizing morsel, and when you get close, you realize too late that it's a monster and the jaws close on you.

To those infatuated with love, Jesus does not chide you; he celebrates the goodness you are experiencing, but then he offers you his cross as the bloody, paradoxical symbol of his love. It challenges that narrow experience of love. Sometimes love is painful.

To those disillusioned with love, Jesus does not shame you; he grieves the pain and loss you feel, but he offers you the very same thing: his cross as the bloody, paradoxical symbol of his love. It consoles you. Sometimes love *is* painful.

The love of God, given to the world in the sacrifice of Jesus and described famously in John 3:16, is *agape* love—unconditionally binding, covenantal love. As Sally Lloyd-Jones put it in her *Jesus Storybook Bible*, it is a "Never Stopping, Never Giving Up, Unbreaking, Always and Forever Love."[5] This is a love that goes beyond warm feelings to something much deeper. It's a love that speaks directly to the skepticism of the disillusioned, offering a binding promise with blood as its proof.

Valentine knew this *agape* love in Jesus, and he offered it to others, even the daughter of his jailer. It was more than words or feelings; it was action—seeking her physical healing, seeking her *good*.

Cyril and Methodius knew this *agape* love, and they offered it to the Slavic people. Not only in feelings, but in genuinely seeking the common good of their culture and society.

True love must be an embodied form of seeking the good of the other. This is the love of God for us in Jesus. Love in a human body seeking our good.

PRAYER

Almighty God, you have surrounded us with a great cloud of witnesses. Grant that we, encouraged by the good example of your servants Valentine, Cyril, and Methodius, may persevere in running the race that is set before us, until at last, with them, we attain to your eternal joy; through Jesus Christ, the pioneer and perfecter of our faith, who lives and reigns with you and the Holy Spirit, one God, forever and ever. Amen.[6]

ARCHBISHOP OF UGANDA AND MARTYR *(c. 1922–1977)*

Commemoration: February 17
Time: Twentieth century
Place: Uganda

While the opportunity is there, I preach the gospel with all my might, and my conscience is clear before God that I have not sided with the present government, which is utterly self-seeking.[1]

UNDER ONE OF THE TWENTIETH CENTURY'S most violent military regimes, Archbishop Janani Luwum laid down his life for Christ and Christ's flock. He became Anglican archbishop in East Africa in 1974, during military dictator Idi Amin's reign of terror. Ugandans were imprisoned, tortured, and murdered for the slightest suspicion of political insubordination. Amin's regime murdered nearly five hundred thousand Ugandans. Janani Luwum had converted to Christianity decades earlier through the influence of the East African revival that had inspired the widespread growth of Christianity in the region. Luwum was known for his passionate preaching, devotion to Jesus Christ, and commitment to the poor and oppressed. He courageously spoke against Amin's abuses despite the risk to his safety. In 1977, Luwum delivered a notice to Amin, protesting arbitrary executions and political kidnappings. This daring defiance led to Luwum's arrest, interrogation, and execution. Before his death, Luwum gave his final words to a friend: "Do not be afraid. I see God's hand in this."

Luwum's courage inspired Ugandan Christians to persevere. The legacy of God's power in the life of Luwum and other Ugandan martyrs is the continued, widespread growth of the church in twenty-first-century Africa. According to a 2005 report from Pew Research Center, "Last Sunday, more Anglicans attended church in each of Kenya, South Africa, Tanzania, and Uganda than did Anglicans in Britain and Canada and Episcopalians in the U.S. combined."[2] This trend continues to escalate in 2024.

SCRIPTURE

> "Then David's anger was greatly kindled against the man, and he said
> to Nathan, 'As the LORD lives, the man who has done this deserves to
> die, and he shall restore the lamb fourfold, because he did this thing,
> and because he had no pity.' Nathan said to David, 'You are the man!'"
> (2 Samuel 12:5-7)

MEDITATION: CONFRONTING THE EMPIRE

It's a relatively new luxury to live in a free society where you can mouth off about the president, the governor, the mayor, or the head of the PTA without fear of the guillotine. This has not always been the case for the people of God. We wax eloquent about the necessity of "speaking truth to power" when all that's at stake is our online reputation, career opportunities, and the awkward dinner with relatives the following year.

Not so for the prophet Nathan. When God sent him to confront King David for his murder of Uriah and the rape of Bathsheba, Nathan likely assumed that he was going to his death. One does not simply walk into Mordor Jerusalem and tell the king that you know his most heinous secrets. Men have died for less. But perhaps to Nathan's surprise, David repented, and Nathan returned to his home.

Many of God's messengers have been sent on similar errands and never returned home again. When Janani Luwum spoke truth to Idi Amin, he may have hoped for a Nathan/David situation. Perhaps the dictator will repent of his evil, turn to the Lord, and amend his ways. Instead Luwum got what usually comes to those who have the courage to open their mouths against political leaders. And those of us today who know his story may find ourselves wondering if we would have the courage to do the same.

But here's a scenario in a different direction: How would you respond if you were confronted with such an accusation? If someone knocked on your door and revealed they knew your worst secret, would you fall to your knees in repentance? Or would you find a way to cover it up? You likely do not have the power to have the messenger's life snuffed out, but you might have the money to bribe them or the leverage to discredit them.

Before we move to confront the empire out there, have we allowed a brother or sister in Christ to confront the empire in here?

PRAYER

Almighty God, we remember this day before you your faithful martyr Janani Luwum, and we pray that, having opened to him the gates of a larger life, you will receive him more and more into your joyful service, that he may win, with you and your servants everywhere, the eternal victory; through Jesus Christ our Lord. Amen.[3]

LUCY YI ZHENMEI, MARTYR OF CHINA *(1815–1862)*

AGNES TSAO KOU YING, MARTYR OF CHINA *(1821–1856)*

AGATHA LIN ZHAO, MARTYR OF CHINA *(1817–1858)*

Commemoration: February 19
Time: Nineteenth century
Place: China

Jesus, save me![1]

CHRISTIANITY REACHED CHINA by the early seventh century and has since experienced many waves of growth and suppression. In the last two hundred years, the Chinese church has grown with unprecedented speed, and Agnes Tsao Kou Ying lived at the beginning of this wave of modern growth. She was born Tsao Kou Ying to a Christian family from Sichuan Province. At age eighteen, she married a farmer and was harassed by her in-laws for her faith. After two years of marriage, her husband died, and she was driven away by her husband's family. A Catholic widow took her into her home and trained her in Scripture and the church's teachings. At Tsao's baptism, she took the name Agnes, after Saint Agnes, a martyr of the ancient church. With the encouragement of a traveling priest, Tsao became a missionary in Guangxi Province. When the government of the Qing dynasty outlawed "wizards, witches, and all superstitions," it extended this prohibition to those practicing Christianity. Tsao was imprisoned and ordered to renounce her faith in Christ. She refused to betray her faith and was locked in a cage so small that she could only stand. For three days, she prayed in the confines of her cage before she died.

Two other Chinese women, Lucy Yi Zhenmei and Agatha Lin Zhao, share similar stories and are commemorated alongside Tsao. Both of these women, also bearing the names of ancient Christian martyrs, were arrested for their Christian faith and beheaded. Their witness, and that of countless other unnamed Chinese Christians, sowed seeds of faith that contributed to an abundant harvest of souls. Today, China is home to one of the largest global populations of Christians, with over sixty-five million believers.[2]

SCRIPTURE

"Remember those who are in prison, as though in prison with them, and those who are mistreated, since you also are in the body." (Hebrews 13:3)

MEDITATION: SOLIDARITY WITH THOSE WHO FEEL TRAPPED

God's people often find their bodies trapped in a cage. Sometimes the bars are made of iron; sometimes they are made of chronic pain, a cancer diagnosis, a misdirected sexual appetite, gender dysphoria, a hostile work environment, a contentious marriage, abusive parents, or overt racism. The feeling of being trapped, incarcerated within your pain, is—unfortunately—not unique to you; it is normal for a follower of Jesus. Taking up your cross to follow Christ often leads to what can feel like a painful dead end.

When we feel trapped in our suffering, it is vital to remember that we never, ever suffer alone. Not only does Jesus himself suffer with us, and not only do we share in the suffering of Christ, but we also share in suffering with one another in the body of the church. The author of Hebrews writes, "as though in prison with them" (Hebrews 13:3). Our siblings are to pray for us with such solidarity that they imagine themselves to be trapped with us. This deep form of empathy is only possible through the Holy Spirit, who flows in, between, and among Christians, binding us in unity.

In the same way, we are to seek this kind of solidarity with those who suffer imprisonment—in any form. Rather than a dismissive, "Too bad for them," or even a heartfelt "I'm so sorry to hear that," we are to cast our imaginations into their lives and seek to view life through their eyes and feel the pain through their bodies. This is difficult; it means intentionally leaving comfort to enter into the suffering of others.

Yet this is exactly what Christ has done for us. Jesus left the comfort, protection, and security of the heavenly realm and condescended to humanity—to see and feel as we see and feel, even when we were in bondage to sin and death. If we know the solidarity of Jesus, then we may seek solidarity with any and all who live trapped in a cage.

PRAYER

Almighty Father, by whose grace and power your holy martyrs Agnes Tsao Kou Ying, Lucy Yi Zhenmei, and Agatha Lin Zhao triumphed over suffering and were faithful even to death: Hasten the coming of your kingdom; and grant that we your servants, who live now by faith, may with joy behold your Son at his coming in glorious majesty; even Jesus Christ, our only Mediator and Advocate. Amen.[3]

BISHOP OF SMYRNA AND MARTYR *(c. 69–c. 155)*

Commemoration: February 23
Time: First and second centuries
Place: Smyrna (now Turkey)

*Eighty and six years have I served [Christ] and he has never abandoned me.
How, then, can I abandon my King and my Savior?*

THE APOSTLE JOHN DISCIPLED several young men who became significant leaders in the early church; among them was Polycarp, who would become the bishop of Smyrna. Polycarp is the author of some of the earliest surviving Christian literature outside of canonical Scripture. His letter to the Philippian church reveals a pastor who masterfully quoted the New Testament Scriptures to comfort and encourage the church. In this single, brief letter, Polycarp referenced seventeen New Testament writings, including those by Matthew, Mark, Luke, John, Paul, and Peter. His letter offers pastoral counsel to men, women, widows, and clergy, aiming to bind the church together in the love preached by Jesus Christ. "Follow the example of the Lord," wrote Polycarp, "firm and unchangeable in faith, loving the brotherhood, cherishing one another, joined together in truth, giving way to one another in the gentleness of the Lord, despising no one."[2] Polycarp would later exhibit this stalwart faith and humility in his martyrdom.

As an old man, Polycarp was treasured as a last living link to the apostles. The Roman authorities knew Polycarp's importance and singled him out to intimidate the church. At age eighty-six, he was arrested, and the Romans demanded that he renounce Christ and worship the emperor. Bound to a stake in an amphitheater in Smyrna, Polycarp boldly refused with these words: "Eighty and six years have I served [Christ] and he has never abandoned me. How, then, can I abandon my King and my Savior?" The account of Polycarp's martyrdom circulated widely, giving Christians the courage to live and die for Christ, emulating this beloved, final witness to the age of the apostles.

SCRIPTURE

"Be strong and courageous. Do not fear or be in dread of them, for it is the LORD your God who goes with you. He will not leave you or forsake you." (Deuteronomy 31:6)

MEDITATION: NEVER ABANDONED

Think of a time when someone promised to do something for you . . . and then didn't come through. How did that feel? All of us have wounds buried deep within that were inflicted not by someone's deliberately wicked act, but simply by their negligence. We might call these "wounds of absence." There are empty gaps, unfilled spaces in our hearts, left there by people we used to count on. If this kind of absence wound becomes the rule rather than the exception, we may begin to displace our pain and disappointment onto God: *God will not be there for me. God has abandoned me.*

When we sink into this kind of despair, we may be tempted to look for comfort in saccharine platitudes or poems about footsteps in the sand; but deep problems require deep solutions. The arrival of the Holy Spirit at Pentecost to indwell the church is not an odd, random chapter in the biblical story, but the fulfillment of what God had promised his people all along. The first disciples felt this transition most acutely. They were with Jesus in the flesh and remembered his statement that it was better for him to leave and send the Holy Spirit.

No doubt, they doubted. We doubt too. Is it really better to have the Spirit than to have Jesus in the flesh? And yet after the ascension of Christ and after Pentecost, we never hear the disciples complain about the good old days when Jesus was with them in his body. Interesting.

The Holy Spirit that comes to dwell within you is God's down payment, his guarantee, that he is committed to us forever. The Spirit fills your wound of absence with the very presence of God.

Therefore, secured and comforted by the sacrifice of Jesus and the indwelling of the Spirit, you can face anything today knowing that God is with you. He will never abandon you.

PRAYER

O God, you strengthened your servant Polycarp in his time of trial and you know that we too are set in the midst of many grave dangers, and because of the frailty of our nature we cannot always stand upright: Grant that your strength and protection may support us in all dangers and carry us through every temptation; through Jesus Christ our Lord, who lives and reigns with you and the Holy Spirit, one God, forever and ever. Amen.[3]

PERPETUA, MARTYR OF AFRICA *(c. 181–c. 203)*
FELICITY, MARTYR OF AFRICA *(?–c. 203)*

Commemoration: March 7
Time: Second and third centuries
Place: Carthage (now Tunisia)

I cannot be called by any other name than what I am—a Christian. **PERPETUA**[1]

[Jesus] will suffer for me. . . . I will be suffering for Him. **FELICITY**[2]

THROUGH THE GOSPEL'S TRANSFORMING POWER, women's perspectives were cherished and elevated by many in the ancient church. One of the most popular writings in the early church was authored by a woman whose first-person narrative showed women and men how to live for Christ in a hostile world.

Perpetua was a noblewoman in the Roman province of Africa (now Tunisia). At twenty-two, a nursing mother and a recent convert to Christianity, she was arrested and thrown into prison, where she met her cellmate, a pregnant enslaved woman named Felicity. Both women, of different social ranks and societal influence, were imprisoned for the same reason: they were Christians who refused to deny Christ. While in prison, Perpetua wrote in her diary, recording the physical and emotional agonies of separation from her baby. Felicity gave birth while in prison. Perpetua, Felicity, and four other Christians were condemned to die in the arena as entertainment for the birthday celebration of the emperor.

Before her death, Perpetua received visions confirming that through the Lord, she would be victorious over Satan. In the first vision, a great ladder stretched before her, reaching into a distant, heavenly garden. A fierce dragon lurked beneath this ladder, trying to terrify all who attempted to climb. "He will not harm me, in the name of Christ Jesus,"[3] said Perpetua. Using the dragon's head as her first step up the ladder, Perpetua ascended into the heavenly garden and met a kindly shepherd who greeted her with the words, "I am glad you have come, my child."[4] In Perpetua's second vision on the eve of her death, she was taken to the amphitheater before an enormous crowd. There, she fought in hand-to-hand combat with a fierce gladiator, but Perpetua was victorious, stepping on the gladiator's head and receiving a branch of victory. "I began to walk in triumph toward the Gate of Life," Perpetua wrote. "Then I awoke. I realized that it was not with wild animals that I would fight but with the Devil, but I knew that I would win the victory."[5] With this final vision, Perpetua finished her diary.

Gladiators and wild animals killed Perpetua, Felicity, and their companions in an African amphitheater. Amid their sufferings, the women gave each other the kiss of peace before being put to the sword. Perpetua's diary account was widely circulated after her death with the title *The Passion of*

Saints Perpetua and Felicity. This document is the oldest surviving Christian literature known to be written by a woman and attests to God's power in granting courage, unity, and confidence to early Christians as they faced unspeakable agonies.

SCRIPTURE

"Blessed are you when others revile you and persecute you and utter all kinds of evil against you falsely on my account. Rejoice and be glad, for your reward is great in heaven, for so they persecuted the prophets who were before you." (Matthew 5:11-12)

MEDITATION: SUFFERING FOR HIS NAME

What is the difference between generic suffering and persecution? Isn't the difference found in the *why* behind the suffering? Often we are guilty of re-branding our suffering as persecution because it buffers us from the idea that we may have brought our pain on ourselves. We don't want to contend with the notion that perhaps our impatience, critical words, or self-centeredness are the real reason someone has ostracized us or hurt us.

Genuine, biblical persecution occurs when you are suffering for the name of Jesus. How can you be sure that you are experiencing genuine persecution for your faith in Jesus? Listen to your enemies, serve your enemies, and sacrifice for the good of your enemies. If you *still* receive hurt from them after seeking their good, then you may very well be experiencing the reality of the beatitude in Matthew 5:11-12. When you experience this kind of pain from the hands of those who hate Christ, you need not be offended or tempted to retaliate. You can realize that their anger (even if they are unaware of it) is directed toward your Savior and not really toward you. You can realize that, in your suffering, you are included in the family of saints, like Perpetua and Felicity, who have been persecuted throughout the long history of the church.

Then, and only then, may you receive the blessing and reward promised by Christ to all who suffer for his name.

PRAYER

Almighty God, you gave your servants Perpetua and Felicity boldness to confess the name of our Savior Jesus Christ before the rulers of this world and courage to die for this faith. Grant that we may always be ready to give a reason for the hope that is in us, and to suffer gladly for the sake of our Lord Jesus Christ, who lives and reigns with you and the Holy Spirit, one God, forever and ever. Amen.[6]

PROPHETIC WITNESS *(c. 1822–1913)*

Commemoration: March 10
Time: Nineteenth and twentieth centuries
Place: United States

God's time is always near. He set the North Star in the heavens;
He gave me the strength in my limbs; He meant I should be free.[1]

HARRIET TUBMAN WAS A VISIONARY and courageous herald of freedom who relied on God for her strength and inspiration. She was born enslaved in Maryland and, from an early age, was subjected to routine cruelty from slaveholders. At age twelve, she received a severe head injury when a slave master, intending to hit another person with an iron weight, missed his target and hit Harriet instead. She suffered from migraines and seizures for the rest of her life. As a teenager, she began to receive visions and strange dreams. Many dismissed these visions as merely side effects of her injury, but Tubman believed them to be revelations from God, who was raising her up as a liberator of his people. Tubman had heard white pastors preach that slaves should be passive and accept their conditions, no matter their cruel circumstances. Tubman was illiterate but was intimately acquainted with the teachings of the Bible and knew that these sermons did not describe the God of Scripture, who delivered the Hebrew slaves out of their bondage in Egypt.

Sustained by her faith, Tubman escaped slavery and fled to Philadelphia in 1849. She then made thirteen heroic trips back to Maryland, personally smuggling over seventy enslaved individuals to freedom (some accounts estimate as many as three hundred were liberated). Tubman brought so many people to freedom that abolitionist allies called her the "conductor of the Underground Railroad," and Tubman was proud to say, "I never lost a passenger."[2] Those who followed her to freedom simply called her Moses. A fellow abolitionist noted that Harriet "talked with God, and he talked with her every day of her life."[3] Tubman said God was her foundation and guiding light through the many dangers she faced. "I said to the Lord, I'm going to hold steady on to you, and I know you'll see me through."[4] During the Civil War, she was a nurse, scout, spy, and military leader. In her later years, she became an advocate for the rights and dignity of women and the elderly and served devotedly in the African Methodist Episcopal Zion Church.

SCRIPTURE

"It was not because you were more in number than any other people that the LORD set his love on you and chose you, for you were the fewest of all peoples, but it is because the LORD loves you and is keeping the oath that he swore to your fathers." (Deuteronomy 7:7-8)

MEDITATION: NO LITTLE PEOPLE

Most of the people who went on to do great things for God were unlikely heroes. Jacob was a liar. Moses was a lousy public speaker. David was the youngest kid in the family. Jonah was racist. Peter was a blue-collar fisherman. Mary Magdalene was tormented by demons. Timothy was too young. If you're looking for recruits to change the world, these would not be top draft picks.

And yet these are the people God chooses. In Deuteronomy 7:7-8, we have a record of the Lord saying to his people that he didn't choose them because they were big and powerful, but rather because he loved them. God loves to use those that the world deems too small, too weak, too insignificant to make a difference. As Francis Schaeffer wrote:

> Consider the mighty ways in which God used a dead stick of wood. . . .
> Though we are limited and weak in talent, physical energy and psychological strength, we are not less than a stick of wood. But as the rod of Moses had to become the rod of God, so that which is me must become the me of God. Then, I can become useful in God's hands. The Scripture emphasizes that much can come from little if the little is truly consecrated to God. There are no little people and no big people in the true spiritual sense, but only consecrated and unconsecrated people. The problem for each of us is applying this truth to ourselves.[5]

J. R. R. Tolkien echoes this theme in his Lord of the Rings trilogy, in which it is the hobbits—the small, peace-loving race of creatures—that bring down the mighty powers of darkness.

Harriet Tubman was an unlikely choice. If you were looking for a liberator to lead a subversive movement to overthrow evil and free the oppressed, wouldn't you pick someone with deep financial resources and, say, an army? Would you pick a slave girl with head trauma? Yet the Lord chose her and used her. And because she was chosen, she was no longer just Harriet, but (to use the phraseology of Francis Schaeffer) the Harriet of God. And this new Harriet was not little, but a giant.

You, dear friend, are not too little, too poor, too stupid, too lost, too messed up, too *anything* to be used by God if you are willing to consecrate yourself—that is, give your whole self over—to him.

PRAYER

Almighty and everlasting God, you kindled the flame of your love in the heart of your servant Harriet Tubman to manifest your compassion and mercy to the poor and the persecuted. Grant to us, your humble servants, a like faith and power of love, that we who give thanks for her righteous zeal may profit by her example, through Jesus Christ our Lord, who lives and reigns with you and the Holy Spirit, one God, forever and ever. Amen.[6]

BISHOP AND MISSIONARY *(c. 385–c. 461)*

Commemoration: March 17
Time: Fourth and fifth centuries
Place: Roman Britain (now England) and Ireland

May Christ be with us. Christ above us. Christ in us. Christ before us.
May your salvation, O Lord, be always ours this day and for evermore.[1]

IRELAND WAS EVANGELIZED by a formerly enslaved young man named Patrick. Patrick escaped to freedom in his homeland of Roman Britannia and never wanted to return. But Patrick believed that true freedom was found in the service of the Lord, and the Lord called him as a minister of mercy to those who had once been his oppressors.

Patrick was born in England during the final years of Roman rule in Britain. He was the son of a deacon and grandson of a priest, but as a young man, he did not take his own faith seriously. In his *Confession*, Patrick recalled, "I did not, indeed, know the true God . . . [nor was I] obedient to our priests who used to remind us of our salvation."[2] At sixteen years old, he was kidnapped by Irish pirates and sold into slavery in pagan Ireland. During six years of slavery, Patrick came to believe that Jesus Christ was his only hope. He repented, converted, and grew in his faith while in captivity. "More and more did the love of God, and my fear of him and faith increase," said Patrick. "The Spirit was burning in me at that time."[3]

In his early twenties, Patrick heard a mysterious voice tell him the time had come to flee his slave master and journey to the coast. A ship was waiting, just as Patrick had been told, and he undertook a harrowing journey back to his native England, where he received a vision of the Irish people calling him with one voice, "We beg you, holy youth, that you shall come and shall walk again among us."

Patrick studied the faith in monasteries in England and mainland Europe and was ordained. He then returned as a missionary to the people who had once enslaved him. "I want to spend myself in that country, even in death, if the Lord should grant me this favor," Patrick wrote in his *Confession*. "It is among that people that I want to wait for the promise made by [the Lord], who assuredly never tells a lie. He makes this promise in the Gospel: 'They shall come from the east and west, and sit down with Abraham, Isaac, and Jacob.' This is our faith: believers are to come from the whole world."[4]

Patrick faced danger from hostile Irish pagans, contending with powerful kings and druids. It was while facing these dangers that Patrick is said to have written his famous prayer of protection, Saint Patrick's Breastplate. This prayer is still prayed by millions of Christians today. With patience and courage, Patrick baptized and shepherded thousands.

SCRIPTURE

"Now the word of the LORD came to Jonah the son of Amittai, saying, 'Arise, go to Nineveh, that great city, and call out against it, for their evil has come up before me.' But Jonah rose to flee to Tarshish from the presence of the LORD." (Jonah 1:1-3)

MEDITATION: HIDE-AND-SEEK

Young children love to play hide-and-seek. If you can playfully say to a child, "I'm gonna get you!" they will run away squealing. But if you pursue them into the room where they are hiding and say, "Now where did they go?" You'll hear a giggle from under a pile of pillows before they spring out and declare, "Here I am!"

This ambivalent dissonance between the desire to hide and the desire to be found does not disappear as we age, it rather becomes darker and more complex. The ways in which we hide become more devious, and our desire to be found becomes more desperate.

The Bible tells the story of people who run and hide and a God who pursues and seeks. This dynamic is on full display in the story of Jonah—which is, I would argue, one of the best short stories (if not *the* best) ever written. It is a masterful tale, simple enough for a child to enjoy and complex enough to devastate an adult.

Jonah ran from God because he realized that God desires to show his grace and mercy to despicable enemies—the Ninevites. God's sending Jonah to Nineveh is like a Jew being sent to Nazi Germany in the 1940s, a Rwandan Tutsi being sent to the Hutus in the 1990s, an Armenian being sent to the Ottomans in the 1910s, or an African being sent to New Orleans in the early 1800s.

Between the storm and the giant fish, Jonah, the runaway prophet, was found by God and recognized it as the Lord's mercy to him. This prepared him to call the Ninevites to stop running from God and to be found by him, even while he was still harboring his own bitterness toward them.

Patrick's return, in contrast, was wholehearted and unreserved. It would have been understandable for Patrick to run from God as well. Why didn't he flee? Why did he return to minister to the very people who had abused and traumatized him? Only a deep, personal experience of God's mercy could have cultivated so generous a heart.

Whom has God called you to serve? Are you still running? Have you been found by God? Have you answered the call to serve those who are still running from God?

PRAYER: SAINT PATRICK'S BREASTPLATE

I bind this day to me forever,
By power of faith, Christ's incarnation;
His baptism in the Jordan River;
His death on cross for my salvation;
His bursting from the spicéd tomb;
His riding up the heavenly way;
His coming at the day of doom
I bind unto myself today.
Christ be with me, Christ within me,
Christ behind me, Christ before me,
Christ beside me, Christ to win me,
Christ to comfort and restore me.
Christ beneath me, Christ above me,
Christ in quiet, Christ in danger,
Christ in hearts of all that love me,
Christ in mouth of friend and stranger.
I bind unto myself today the name,
The strong name of the Trinity,
By invocation of the same,
The Three in One, and One in Three,
Of whom all nature hath creation,
Eternal Father, Spirit, Word;
Praise to the Lord of my salvation,
Salvation is of Christ the Lord. Amen.[5]

ARCHBISHOP OF EL SALVADOR AND MARTYR *(1917–1980)*

Commemoration: March 24
Time: Twentieth century
Place: El Salvador

An accommodating church… that seeks prestige without the pain of the cross, is not the authentic church of Jesus Christ.[1]

ÓSCAR ROMERO SERVED CHRIST amid the clashing agendas of the Cold War. He was archbishop of El Salvador during a violent civil war between the military-led government and revolutionary guerrillas. Rival Cold War powers funded each side of the war and intensified its fury.

Romero was once known for his cautious and conservative approach to ministry, but this changed with the outbreak of widespread violence. Thousands of impoverished people cried out against both the government and the guerrillas and were subsequently imprisoned or murdered. Seeing these evils, Romero was compelled to speak boldly for human rights and the poor. "Let's say to everyone," said Romero, "we must take the cause of the poor seriously, as if it were our own cause, or even more, for it is indeed the very cause of Jesus Christ."[2]

Romero's courageous defense of the poor earned him many powerful enemies on all sides of the conflict. His critiques of Marxism challenged many revolutionaries. "If one understands by 'Marxism' a materialistic, atheistic ideology that is taken to explain the whole of human existence and gives a false interpretation of religion," Romero said, "then it is completely untenable by a Christian."[3]

Allies of the government opposed Romero for his forceful preaching against the status quo. "A church that doesn't provoke any crises," said Romero, "a gospel that doesn't unsettle, a word of God that doesn't get under anyone's skin, a word of God that doesn't touch the real sin of the society in which it is being proclaimed—what gospel is that?"[4]

Government allies were also threatened by Romero's stand against injustice in the government and military. After a military slaughter of men, women, and children in March 1980, Romero preached a powerful sermon calling on soldiers to abandon their posts. "No soldier is obliged to obey an order contrary to the law of God. No one has to obey an immoral law. . . . I implore you, I beg you, I order you in the name of God: stop the repression."[5] The next day, Romero was in a hospital chapel to celebrate Mass. As he stood at the altar, a government agent entered the room and shot Romero to death. Chaos and violence continued, even at Romero's funeral, where smoke bombs went off and gunfire broke out amid the ceremony of over 250,000 attendees. A delegate from Pope John Paul II eulogized Romero during the ceremony. Despite the chaos in El Salvador still evident at the funeral, the eulogist's message was one of hope, calling Romero a "beloved, peacemaking man of God . . . [whose] blood will give fruit to brotherhood, love and peace."[6]

SCRIPTURE

> "Blessed are the peacemakers, for they shall be called sons of God."
> (Matthew 5:9)

MEDITATION: THE WAR OF EVERYONE AGAINST EVERYONE

Thomas Hobbes, a seventeenth-century English philosopher, wrote, "*Bellum omnium contra omnes*," a Latin phrase meaning "the war of all against all" or "the war of everyone against everyone." Hobbes describes this as the natural state of humanity—a state of continual fear.[7]

Fear is underneath all conflict. Fear of not being enough, fear of being left out, fear of being taken advantage of, fear of being the wrong kind of person, fear of being victimized, fear of losing your cherished way of life.

Our news media outlets are fear factories. The way to get clicks and sell ad space is to prey on people's fear. There's a lot of money to be made in making people afraid. If you're willing to stoke people's fear, you can get candidates elected and sell people things they don't want or need.

All conflict is rooted in fear, and since perfect love is the antidote to fear (1 John 4:8), all peacemaking must be rooted in love. In other words, true peacemaking in the way of Jesus must not be rooted in fear of conflict. To be a peacemaker is actually not a very peace-*ful* vocation. Peacemakers move toward conflict, but they do so motivated by the love of Christ. Therein lies the crucial difference between peace*keeping* and peace*making*. Peacekeeping fears conflict and seeks to maintain the status quo, often at the expense of truth-telling and justice. Peacemaking does not fear conflict and therefore does not fear to tell the truth and seek justice. Peacekeeping is surface-level homeostasis. Peacemaking is more like surgery to remove a malignant tumor—invasive and often painful.

The gospel paradox of peace is that the cross—a historic symbol of conflict, war, torture, and violence—is now, for us, a symbol of peace. To make peace in the way of Jesus is, therefore, always for the good of the other at a cost to the self. Peacemaking requires sacrifice. It did for Jesus; it does for us too. Óscar Romero was a peacemaker in the way of Jesus, and thus his life was filled with conflict and ended in violence.

Peacemaking is now part of the vocation of all Christians. Peacemaking is living out the shalom of the new creation, starting now. Frederick Bauerschmidt, professor at Loyola University, has written, "If Thomas Hobbes is wrong and the book of Genesis is right, then human reconciliation with God, our return to the natural state of things, is inseparable from our reconciliation with each other. To end the war of humanity against God is to end the war of everyone against everyone."[8]

What conflict is disrupting your corner of the world? Where might you, motivated by love (and not fear), enter that conflict as a peacemaker in the way of Jesus?

PRAYER

Almighty God, you created us in your own image. Grant us, inspired by the witness of your servant Óscar Romero, grace to contend fearlessly against evil and to make no peace with oppression; and help us to use our freedom rightly in the establishment of justice in our communities and among the nations, to the glory of your holy name, through Jesus Christ our Lord, who lives and reigns with you and the Holy Spirit, one God, now and forever. Amen.[9]

HERMIT *(c. 344–c. 421)*

Commemoration: April 1
Time: Fourth and fifth centuries
Place: Egypt and Palestine

When I only reflect on the evils from which our Lord has delivered me, I have imperishable food for hope of salvation. I am fed and clothed by the all-powerful word of God, the Lord of all.[1]

MARY OF EGYPT WAS ONCE ANGRY AT GOD and filled with hatred for his creatures. But this great sinner was loved by an even greater Savior, and she was miraculously transformed into a glorious new creation. She was born in Egypt and, at age twelve, ran away from home. For seventeen years, she lived as a beggar and prostitute, consumed by hatred and lust. According to Mary, "Every kind of abuse of nature I regarded as life." Desiring to undermine the souls of others, she journeyed to Jerusalem in a perverse antipilgrimage, to draw Christian pilgrims off their path and into sexual debasement. "I am amazed ... how it was that hell did not swallow me alive when I had entangled in my net so many souls," Mary recalled. "But I think God was seeking my repentance. For He does not desire the death of a sinner."[2]

In Jerusalem, she encountered the Church of the Holy Sepulchre, which housed Christ's empty tomb and the relics of the holy cross. Seeing crowds of pilgrims entering the church doors, she was seized by a strong desire to enter with them. But no matter how hard she tried to enter, a mysterious, unseen force barred her way. Suddenly she was struck to the heart, realizing the depth of her sin. She then saw an icon of the blessed virgin Mary outside the church. The sight of this very different Mary, who fully submitted herself to the love and will of God, brought Mary of Egypt to repentance and faith. She was baptized and assured of God's forgiveness for her sins. Leaving Jerusalem, she journeyed into the wilderness on the far side of the Jordan River, where she lived a life of repentance, fasting, and prayer.

Many decades later, a monk named Zosimas wandered deep into the wilderness. At a distance, he spotted a mysterious figure, which, at first, he mistook to be the devil. The figure was thin, skin darkened by the burning sun, and hair bleached white. It was Mary, now an old woman. She humbly recounted her life story to Zosimas, which he wrote down in a document called *The Life of Mary of Egypt*. She spoke of God's grace saving her, a "miserable wretch." She begged Zosimas for his prayers and asked that he bring her the Eucharist during the next Holy Week. Zosimas obliged. He returned to the Jordan River at the time Mary requested. Mary approached from the far side of the Jordan, miraculously walking across the water to receive the bread and wine. Once she had received Christ's body and blood, she vanished into the wilderness, never to be seen alive again. Her body was found by Zosimas a year later, with her arms crossed over her chest. She was fully resigned to the will of her loving Father, peacefully received into the eternal life of the one who does not desire the death of a sinner.

SCRIPTURE

"And you were dead in the trespasses and sins in which you once walked, following the course of this world, following the prince of the power of the air, the spirit that is now at work in the sons of disobedience—among whom we all once lived in the passions of our flesh, carrying out the desires of the body and the mind, and were by nature children of wrath, like the rest of mankind. But God, being rich in mercy, because of the great love with which he loved us, even when we were dead in our trespasses, made us alive together with Christ— by grace you have been saved." (Ephesians 2:1-5)

MEDITATION: NO NEUTRAL GROUND

Many faith stories are gentle, and this is a good thing. Many people who become true followers of Jesus do so because they were raised by godly parents, nurtured by faithful churches, and gradually became aware of their need for the redemptive work of Christ.

But sometimes faith stories hinge on a dramatic, even violent, conversion. These stories are crucial not only for those who live them, but for those whose paths have been gentler. The intense conversion stories are sacramental in nature. They reveal and unmask in the physical realm what is always true about us in the spiritual realm.

Consider the apostle Paul's conversion. One moment he was actively persecuting Christians, seeking their destruction. Then, after an encounter with Jesus on the road to Damascus, he began a life of humble submission to the will of the one he formerly hated. This seismic shift from enemy to servant becomes a true mark of conversion. It signifies to us that, when it comes to one's relationship and orientation to Jesus, there is no neutral ground. All humans either wage war as enemies of God or humbly submit as servants. Even those who seek an agnostic life of vague uncertainty and indifference to Christ are, in their passivity, complicit in evil. You might imagine a Russian citizen claiming neutrality as millions died during the extermination of the kulaks in the Soviet Union from the 1910s to the 1930s. Silence implies consent. Passivity is akin to endorsement.

So it is with God. Mary of Egypt's conversion shows us in dramatic fashion what it looks like to change sides, to renounce the life of enmity and embrace the life of submission. The depth of Mary's evil was, in a moment, transformed into a depth of repentance. Thus her conversion plumbed the deep fathoms of her soul. She knew that the very core of her being had hated God, and so in encountering Christ's mercy, she submitted to God all the way down to the core.

Have you converted? If so, how deep has your conversion gone? Does the very core of your soul submit to God, or are there interior rooms that still function as fiercely defended bunkers of rebellion against God? What would your life look like if your conversion went as deep as Paul's or Mary's?

PRAYER

Dear Lord and Savior Jesus Christ, inspired by the life of your servant Mary of Egypt, I hold up all my weakness to your strength, my failure to your faithfulness, my sinfulness to your perfection, my loneliness to your compassion, my little pains to your great agony on the cross. I pray that you will cleanse me, strengthen me, and guide me, so that in all ways my life may be lived as you would have it lived, without cowardice and for you alone. Show me how to live in true humility, true contrition, and true love. Amen.[3]

RENEWER OF SOCIETY *(1929–1968)*

Commemoration: April 4
Time: Twentieth century
Place: United States

Man cannot save himself, for man is not the measure of all things and humanity is not God. Bound by the chains of his own sin and finiteness, man needs a Savior.[1]

THE HEART OF THE TWENTIETH-CENTURY CIVIL RIGHTS MOVEMENT was the faith and prophetic voice of the African American church, and Baptist pastor Martin Luther King Jr. became emblematic of this Christian movement. He was born in Atlanta, Georgia, the son of the senior pastor of Ebenezer Baptist Church. Witnessing his father's stand against discrimination, King was inspired to his own calling. Through his teen years and as a college student, King became skeptical about the faith of his upbringing. Many of his writings as a young adult express this skepticism. But while in college, King found a spiritual and intellectual mentor in the pacifist civil rights activist and Baptist pastor Benjamin Mays. Mays helped direct King toward the legitimacy of the church, the church's teachings, and its power in answering modern societal questions.

King would go on to serve as a pastor in Montgomery, Alabama, and eventually as copastor of Ebenezer Baptist Church in Atlanta. He rose to national prominence in 1955, after Rosa Parks was arrested in Montgomery for refusing to give up her bus seat to a white man. This prompted King and other Christian leaders to help organize a boycott of the bus lines. As the civil rights era unfolded in the 1950s and 1960s, King became one of his generation's most eloquent leaders. He was frequently jailed, he was stabbed nearly to death, his home was bombed, and he was subjected to government surveillance and character assassination attempts. On April 4, 1968, he was shot and killed on the balcony of his Memphis motel room.

During his short life, King was inspired by the words and actions of Jesus, to call the oppressed to remain steadfast in nonviolent resistance, to refuse hatred of one's enemies, and to promote love of neighbor. He urged his society to bring about the works of justice and mercy necessary to affirm the equal dignity and value of every human being. "By opening our lives to God in Christ, we become new creatures," said King. "This experience, which Jesus spoke of as the new birth, is essential if we are to be transformed nonconformists.... Only through an inner spiritual transformation do we gain the strength to fight vigorously the evils of the world in a humble and loving spirit."[2]

SCRIPTURE

"Do not be conformed to this world, but be transformed by the renewal of your mind, that by testing you may discern what is the will of God, what is good and acceptable and perfect." (Romans 12:2)

MEDITATION: THE MORAL IMAGINATION

I have written elsewhere, "From the imagination springs desires; from desires flow actions, which over time wear grooves into habits; from habits develop beliefs that justify; and from beliefs come doctrine. Therefore, if you wish to destroy a faith, strike first not at doctrine; rather, starve the imagination, and doctrine will eventually wither away on its own. Conversely, if you wish to ignite faith, do not begin by teaching doctrine didactically; rather, begin by firing up the imagination."[3]

King was a teacher, but his legacy is not his teaching. King was an activist, but his legacy is not primarily his activism. King was a pastor, but his legacy is not his pastoring. What is the legacy of King? For what is he most remembered? These words: *"I have a dream . . ."* Why? They are words that speak directly of and to the imagination.

We homo sapiens live out of our imaginations. What we imagine to be good, beautiful, true, and desirable is what orients us. We are creatures who require a vision of the good life if we are to get out of bed and go to work.

The Lord knows this, which is why his word to us is mostly story, poetry, song, and apocalypse. What's more, this is why the Word made flesh in Jesus is essential to our transformation. Only when the vision for the good and beautiful life is *embodied* do our imaginations wake up and pay attention.

For this reason, the apostle Paul writes in Romans 12:2, "Be transformed by the renewal of your mind." This is not primarily a command to be changed through learning new information, but rather a call for renewal of imagination.

On Monday evening, January 30, 1956, King received word (in the middle of a church service) that his home had been bombed with his wife, Coretta, and his daughter Yolanda inside. He rushed home and found that, though the front of the house had caved in from the explosion, his wife and daughter were unharmed, though terribly shaken and frightened. Outside, a large, angry crowd had formed and threatened retaliation for this attack on their beloved pastor and leader. King stepped out onto the ruins of his front porch, raised his hands, and with calm but firm voice said, "Everything is all right. Don't get panicky. Don't do anything panicky. Don't get your weapons. If you have weapons, take them home. He who lives by the sword will perish by the sword. Remember that is what Jesus said. We are not advocating violence. We want to love our enemies. I want you to love our enemies. Be good to them. This is what we must live by. We must meet hate with love."[4]

What was happening in that moment? Pastoral care? Yes. Peacemaking? Yes. But more than these, it was a moment of moral imagination. If one had the eyes to see and the ears to hear, it was a transformation moment, a renewal of the mind moment.

What dream are you dreaming? Do you have a vision for a good and beautiful life? If so, where did it come from? What images, words, and visions shape your own imagination? Do you dream the dreams of Jesus? Or are you still trying to get Jesus on board with your dreams?

PRAYER

O God, who created all peoples in your image and raised up your servant Martin Luther King Jr., as a voice of reconciliation: we thank you for the diversity of races and cultures in this world. Show us your presence in those who differ from us, and enrich our lives with their fellowship, until our knowledge of your love is made perfect in our love for all your children, through Jesus Christ our Lord. Amen.[5]

PASTOR AND MARTYR *(1906–1945)*

Commemoration: April 9
Time: Twentieth century
Place: Germany

Lord Jesus Christ, you were poor and in distress, a captive and forsaken as I am.
You know man's troubles; you abide with me.
When all men fail me, you remember and seek me.[1]

DIETRICH BONHOEFFER STOOD AGAINST Hitler and the Nazi regime and refused to give up on Christianity and the German people at the cost of his life. He grew up in Germany and in 1930 moved to New York City to study theology. There, he ministered in Harlem, teaching Sunday school at Abyssinian Baptist Church. Bonhoeffer came to love this African American community and became sensitive to the injustices experienced by ethnic minorities. When Bonhoeffer returned to Germany just before the ascent of Adolf Hitler, German mainline churches were co-opted by Hitler and turned into Nazi political cults, where swastikas replaced crosses and National Socialism replaced orthodox Christianity. Bonhoeffer saw a nation of German Christians willing to compromise the fundamentals of faith because of an abstract belief in "grace." This grace, Bonhoeffer argued, was cheap grace. "Cheap grace is preaching forgiveness without requiring repentance, baptism without church discipline, Communion without confession," Bonhoeffer wrote. "Cheap grace is grace without discipleship, grace without the cross, grace without Jesus Christ, living and incarnate."[2] Bonhoeffer became a leader in an underground Christian community that included a seminary and a network of churches. In his book *The Cost of Discipleship*, Bonhoeffer advocated for "costly grace" to be incarnated into the lives of the Christians in his community. "Costly grace confronts us as a gracious call to follow Jesus. . . . It is costly because it compels a man to submit to the yoke of Christ and follow him; it is grace because Jesus says: 'My yoke is easy and my burden is light.'"

Bonhoeffer boldly lived out costly grace when he spoke against the genocide of Jews, euthanasia, and the suppression of Christianity. Many encouraged Bonhoeffer to wait out the war in the United States, but Bonhoeffer insisted he must remain amid the dangers of Nazi Germany. "I will have no right to participate in the reconstruction of Christian life in Germany after the war if I do not share the trials of this time with my people."[3] By 1943, Bonhoeffer's outspoken boldness had attracted the attention of Nazi authorities. In April 1943, he was arrested and sent to the Flossenbürg prison camp, where he was executed on April 9, 1945, less than a month before the end of the war.

SCRIPTURE

"How good and pleasant it is when brothers dwell in unity!" (Psalm 133:1)

MEDITATION: WHEN THE WISH DREAM DIES

Nearly every person who has darkened the door of a church sanctuary is looking for community. Our human craving for meaningful relationships is a vital aspect of our built-in *imago Dei*, because community is native to the Holy Trinity—eternal relational harmony among Father, Son, and Holy Spirit. When God said, "It is not good that the man should be alone" (Genesis 2:18), it applies to more than married folks; it applies to us all!

The church is the new humanity, of which Christ Jesus is the firstborn. The redemptive community embodied and offered by the people of Jesus is unparalleled in human history: a community established in love, marked by grace, and sustained by mercy.

And yet is this our experience of church? Why are our experiences of community with other Christians so disappointing? Bonhoeffer writes,

> Innumerable times a whole Christian community has broken down because it had sprung up from a wish dream. The serious Christian, set down for the first time in a Christian community, is likely to bring with him a very definite idea of what Christian life together should be and to try to realize it. But God's grace speedily shatters such dreams.... The sooner this shock of disillusionment comes to an individual and to a community the better for both.[4]

He wrote this in reflection on his experience of organizing a clandestine seminary at Finkenwalde. If ever there is an idealistic group of Christians, it is young seminarians! Bonhoeffer went on to write, "When the morning mists of dreams vanish, then dawns the bright day of Christian fellowship."[5]

In other words, true community does not begin until the fantasy dies. This dynamic is true in marriage, it's true in parenting, it's true in friendship, it's true in every relationship. You cannot truly love the real person in front of you until you let go of the imaginary person you want them to be.

What is your wish dream for community, and has it died yet? Perhaps you have a beautiful dream for communal harmony, in the way of King. Might you remember that the ideal of his dream did not cause him to be *idealistic* toward the very real and broken humans with whom he lived and worked. Who are the real brothers and sisters in Christ that are proximate to you? Regardless of their ability to measure up to your ideal, they *are* your Christian community.

PRAYER

Most loving Father, who faithfully abided with your servant Dietrich Bonhoeffer in his suffering and anxiety: you will us to give thanks for all things, to dread nothing but the loss of you, and to cast all our care on the One who cares for us. Grant that no clouds of this mortal life may hide from us the light of that love which is immortal, and which you have manifested unto us in your Son, Jesus Christ our Lord. Amen.[6]

PROPHETIC WITNESS *(1656–1680)*

Commemoration: April 17
Time: Seventeenth century
Place: Iroquois Confederacy (now New York, United States)

My decision . . . has been made.
I have consecrated myself entirely to Jesus, son of Mary.[1]

OF THE MANY INDIGENOUS AMERICAN SAINTS commemorated in the church calendar, Kateri Tekakwitha is remembered for her faithful prayers on behalf of her people. She was born in the Mohawk village of Ossernenon in the region now called upstate New York. Her father was a Mohawk chief, and her mother was an Algonquin captive who had converted to Catholicism. When Tekakwitha was four years old, a smallpox epidemic devastated her village. Tekakwitha and her family caught the disease, and she was the only survivor, left an orphan with diminished eyesight and a scarred face.[2] She was adopted by relatives who, because of her damaged eyesight, named her Tekakwitha, meaning "She who bumps into things."

At age eleven, Tekakwitha met French Jesuit missionaries whose conduct made a deep impression on the young girl. When the Mohawks defeated the Mohican invaders, the prisoners were often subjected to extreme cruelty. At great risk to themselves, the "Blackrobes" (the Mohawk name for Jesuit priests) pled for mercy for the captives. Tekakwitha was compelled by the Blackrobes' gentle compassion and mercy and studied their example throughout her teenage years. With the guidance of a Jesuit priest, she became a Christian and was baptized. At her baptism, she was given the name Kateri, a form of the name Catherine, in honor of Catherine of Siena. Tekakwitha had long avoided marriage and committed herself entirely to the Lord's service. "For a long time, my decision on what I will do has been made," she said. "I have consecrated myself entirely to Jesus, son of Mary, I have chosen Him for husband, and He alone will take me for wife."

The Mohawks interpreted Tekakwitha's new faith as sorcery and mistreated her. Children threw stones at her, she was refused food, and she became the village outcast. Eventually, she was forced to flee her homeland, along with other Christian converts, to live in a Jesuit mission south of Montreal. She devoted the rest of her life to prayer and fasting for her people. She was known for making simple wooden crosses as she prayed, and she filled the forests around the Jesuit mission with these testaments of her faith.

SCRIPTURE

"You shall be holy, for I the LORD your God am holy." (Leviticus 19:2)

MEDITATION: A HOLY LIFE

When we hear the word *holy*, we tend to think of someone with preeminent virtue, bordering on self-righteous piety. The phrase "holier than thou" comes to mind. For this reason, few Christians desire holiness. To say, "I want to be holy," sounds like saying, "I want to be better than other people." Holiness sounds like the opposite of humility.

But words have meanings, even if people misuse them. Holy does not mean better, it means "set apart" or "consecrated." A holy object is something that is set apart for a special purpose. Consider the temple worship of ancient Israel. The Levitical priests made use of all sorts of instruments and tools for worship: pots, cups, staffs, knives, etc. These were holy objects. The holy cups used in the temple were not "better" cups, they were simply cups set aside for the special purpose of corporate worship. The opposite of holy is not bad; the opposite of holy is ordinary. Example: if you're an ancient Israelite, you have your ordinary, everyday kitchen knives, and then you have the holy knife used for temple sacrifices.

The same is true for people. A holy person is not superior; rather they are someone whose life is set aside for a special purpose. Most people live ordinary lives. Ordinary lives are not bad lives; they're just common, normal. A holy life is a life set apart from the ordinary. The process of setting apart an ordinary object or person to be holy is called consecration. To consecrate is to "holi-fy" something or someone. When a priest celebrates the Eucharist in a Christian worship service, ordinary bread and wine are consecrated and become holy. They still have all the markings of bread and wine, but they are no longer ordinary or common. They now have the special purpose of being the Lord's Supper.

Kateri consecrated her life to Jesus, making her whole self available for God's use.

How much of your life have you made available to God for his use, his purposes, his mission? Are there parts of your life that you have withheld from God, afraid of what he might ask you to do?

PRAYER

O God, the light of the minds that know you, the life of the souls that love you, and the strength of the wills that serve you, just as you brought your daughter Kateri Tekakwitha to the light of love, help us so to know you that we may truly love you, and so to love you that we may fully serve you, whom to serve is perfect freedom, through Jesus Christ our Lord. Amen.[3]

REFORMER OF THE CHURCH *(1347–1380)*

Commemoration: April 29
Time: Fourteenth century
Place: Italy

Be who God meant you to be, and you will set the world on fire.[1]

IN A WORLD CRUMBLING FROM disease, war, and societal upheaval, God empowered a young woman to become a powerful voice of reform, mercy, and love. Catherine of Siena was born into a world ravaged by the Black Death, the Hundred Years' War, and deep-seated political corruption in the church. From a young age, Catherine witnessed profound visions of Jesus. Despite her parents' wishes, she refused marriage and spent most of her time in prayer and contemplation in the basement of her family's home.

Catherine emerged at age twenty-one, having been commanded by the Lord to enter public life. At first, this command meant re-engaging with family members and caring for the poor in her neighborhood. Soon her ministry expanded, and Catherine became a prophetic voice on political, social, and global church matters. Through a rare combination of strong conviction and humility, she spoke out against clerical corruption, denounced insurrectionist political movements, and called for aid for Christians suffering in the Middle East. "O alas, be silent no more!" Catherine wrote. "Shout with a hundred thousand tongues. I see that, through silence, the world is broken, the Bride of Christ has turned pale."[2] She wrote letters to kings, queens, and bishops, boldly calling them to reform. In the fourteenth century, popes of Rome resided in Avignon, France, where for seventy years they enjoyed political favors and protection. Catherine worked to end this long "Babylonian captivity" of the papacy. She journeyed to Avignon and petitioned Pope Gregory XI, calling on him to return to Rome. Catherine spoke before cardinals and bishops, urging them to preserve the church's integrity and end the season of corruption and confusion. She died at age thirty-three, exhausted from her rigorous service for the Lord.

Catherine's life disproves the common assumption that only ordained clergy can speak boldly within the kingdom of God. Catherine is now considered a doctor of the church, an exclusive title given to a small number of saints who made particularly significant contributions to theology and doctrine. Catherine was the first laywoman to receive this prestigious distinction.

SCRIPTURE

"And they remembered his words, and returning from the tomb they told all these things to the eleven and to the all the rest. Now it was

Mary Magdalene and Joanna and Mary the mother of James and the other women with them who told these things to the apostles, but these words seemed to them an idle tale, and they did not believe them." (Luke 24:8-11)

MEDITATION: HEARING THE VOICES OF WOMEN

The very first people to proclaim the resurrection of Jesus were women. Mary Magdalene, Joanna, Mary the mother of James, and other women found the empty tomb and had an encounter with the risen Christ. They returned to the disciples with the astonishing news, only to be dismissed as hysterical women. At that time in history, not only were women viewed as inherently inferior to men, but women were rarely permitted to testify in court, because (in the social imagination of the time) who would trust the word of a woman?

Sadly, much of church history bears the tragic tale of women disbelieved, demeaned, and discouraged. Many (not all) Christians are reclaiming, from Christ and the first-century church, the belief that women are coequal with men in dignity, value, and personhood, but the church has a long way to go to fully embrace this gospel vision. And yet—*and yet!*—the consistent witness of history is that the Christian faith is *good* for women. Everywhere the church has spread, women are more elevated, protected, and valued than they were before.

History is complicated. Has the church often suppressed the voices of women? Yes. Have the non-Christian cultures and societies of the world oppressed women to an even greater degree? Again, yes.

The solution to the oppression of women is not found outside the church, but rather in the fullness of what the church was always meant to be. We see this in the way Jesus himself dignified, elevated, and encouraged women, and we see it in the impact that women like Catherine of Siena had on the world in her time. Thank goodness for those few who listened to Catherine! What if they had all dismissed her as a hysterical woman? The world would have missed benefiting from her wisdom.

When the church practices the way of her Lord, the voices of women are heard and believed on the merit of what they have to say, and this bears good fruit—both for the church and for the world.

If you are part of a local church, where are the voices of women invited, listened to, and believed on merit? Are there any areas where women's voices are not invited? With the patience, grace, and gentleness of Jesus, where might you create venues where women's voices are invited and dignified in new ways?

PRAYER

O God, inspired by the witness of your servant Catherine of Siena, we pray: take our minds and think through them. Take our lips and speak through them. Take our hearts and set them on fire with love for you. What we know not, teach us. What we have not, give us. What we are not, make us. For Jesus Christ's sake. Amen.[3]

RENEWER OF SOCIETY AND
TRANSLATOR OF THE BIBLE *(1858–1922)*

Commemoration: April 30
Time: Nineteenth and twentieth centuries
Place: India

A life totally committed to God has nothing to fear,
nothing to lose, nothing to regret.[1]

JESUS GIVES DIGNITY TO ALL PEOPLE, and he inspired Pandita Ramabai in her outspoken advocacy for voiceless Indian women. In her day, Indian society was divided into a fixed hierarchy of castes, and women of all castes were expected to exist in the background. Girls, often younger than ten years old, were given in marriage to much older men. Young widows were considered cursed, their heads were shaved, and they suffered abuse.[2] Women across India silently faced injustice and were denied education and autonomy. Ramabai wanted to put an end to all of this, and her inspiration began as a child, with the encouragement of her father.

Ramabai's father was a Hindu member of a high-caste Brahmin family. Defying cultural norms, he refused to marry off his daughter at a young age and personally taught her Sanskrit, a sacred Hindu language intended only for highest-caste men. He also gave Ramabai a comprehensive education in literature, religion, and science. When Ramabai was sixteen years old, her father and mother died from famine, and she was forced to support herself in Calcutta, reciting Sanskrit literature. She attracted attention as she demonstrated her education and became known as a Pandita (scholar) by teachers at the University of Calcutta.

In her twenties, Ramabai created scandal by marrying and having a child with a man of a lower caste. After only two years, her husband died. Now a widow, she once again did the unthinkable: she traveled across the globe as a single mother. In England, she taught Sanskrit and Marathi (one of the national languages of India). She cherished her Indian heritage but searched for a philosophy that did not degrade women. While in England, she heard the gospel of Jesus. "Having lost all faith in my former religion," Ramabai said, "and with my heart hungering after something better, I eagerly learnt everything I could about the Christian religion, and declared my intention to become a Christian.... I realized, after reading the fourth chapter of St. John's Gospel, that Christ was truly the Divine Savior he claimed to be, and no one but He could transform and uplift the downtrodden women of India.... Thus my heart was drawn to the religion of Christ."[3]

Many Indians resented Ramabai for embracing Christianity and for giving herself the name Mary to mark her baptism. She clashed with Westerners for protesting colonialist attitudes, wearing Indian clothing, and eating a vegetarian diet. Keeping her eyes fixed on Jesus' example, she established communities for homeless Indian women and children and wrote and spoke for the voiceless women of India. She translated the Bible from Hebrew and Greek into Marathi, allowing Indian men and women to hear and read God's Word in their native tongue. Her translation, like her life work, transformed and uplifted her people through the hope found only in Jesus Christ.

SCRIPTURE

"For I the LORD love justice; I hate robbery and wrong; I will faithfully give them their recompense, and I will make an everlasting covenant with them." (Isaiah 61:8)

MEDITATION: JUSTICE AS A CLUE TO THE MEANING OF THE UNIVERSE

C. S. Lewis begins *Mere Christianity* with a chapter titled "Right and Wrong as a clue to the meaning of the universe," making a compelling case that human moral instinct is evidence of God's existence. Today, words like *right* and *wrong* are out of fashion, so when N. T. Wright begins his book *Simply Christian*, he uses the same logic as Lewis but updates the language: "Justice as a clue to the meaning of the universe."

When humans express moral indignation, we are saying something about the way things ought to be, and there cannot be an *ought* without there being *intention*. This is a breadcrumb, a signpost, that there is a Great Intention behind and underneath all that exists. Meerkats do not express moral outrage when a hyena devours a litter of pups, but humans cry out in righteous protest when an active shooter mows down a kindergarten classroom. It is wrong. It is *evil*. We know it in our guts. This is not the way things ought to be.

But why? The search for a rationale behind our human justice instinct is a pathway to discovering the God of the Bible. No other faith can make sense of suffering and offer a genuine solution to the injustice of this world. The Christian faith tells a story about justice:

- Creation: The world was made for goodness, peace, and shalom. (This is why we all have a sense of the way things ought to be.)

- Fall: The world has been corrupted and broken by sin. (This is why injustice, suffering, and pain are a plague on the world.)

- Redemption: Jesus has taken the corruption of sin on himself and put it to death. (This is how God has enacted a solution where he bears the responsibility for what humans have caused.)

- Consummation: One day all things will be made new, and shalom will reign forever. (This is the guaranteed hope that gives us endurance, patience, and even joy as we labor for justice in this life.)

Ramabai longed for justice for her people but could not find support for this longing in her Hindu religion. This sent her on a journey toward Jesus and the Christian faith, where she found both a satisfying explanation of the world and clarity on how to pursue justice for others.

We live in a cultural moment where so many people feel a heightened need for social justice. This movement flows out of the justice instincts that are hardwired into every human heart. The opportunity that lies before the church is to helpfully clarify what this longing for justice means and to become a signpost that points people toward the source of true justice, Jesus himself.

Do you know non-Christians who burn with passion for justice? Do you know that a passion for justice is a wonderful point of commonality that Christians and non-Christians may experience in their shared humanity? How might you help your neighbors see that their longing for justice is evidence that God has made this world for good and that he intends to restore it one day?

PRAYER

O God, who showed forth the light of your gospel in the land of India through your faithful servant Pandita Mary Ramabai, enlighten our hearts, that we may receive with faith your promises, and so be numbered with your saints in glory everlasting, through Jesus Christ our Lord. Amen.[4]

"EVEN ON THE CROSS, HE DID NOT HIDE HIMSELF FROM SIGHT; RATHER, HE MADE ALL CREATION WITNESS TO THE PRESENCE OF ITS MAKER."

BISHOP of ALEXANDRIA & TEACHER of the FAITH

ἀθανάσιος

ATHAN-ASIUS c. 296-373

ὁμοούσιον

BISHOP OF ALEXANDRIA AND TEACHER OF THE FAITH *(c. 296–373)*

Commemoration: May 2
Time: Fourth century
Place: Egypt

Even on the cross, he did not hide himself from sight; rather, he made all creation witness to the presence of its maker.[1]

WHO IS JESUS? Is he God, the Creator of all things? Or is he more of a divine hero—a human who became God by grace? Was there a time when Jesus did not exist? In the fourth century, many Christians sought answers to questions like these. A young African deacon named Athanasius played an important role in bringing biblical clarity to these questions.

Athanasius was born to Christian parents in Egypt. As a child, he witnessed some of his Christian tutors martyred for their beliefs, but this did not dampen Athanasius's faith. The Scriptures captivated his imagination and as a young man he wrote *On the Incarnation*, a profound reflection on the ancient teaching that the eternal God became man in the person of Jesus. The bishop of Alexandria soon became aware of Athanasius's gifts and ordained him a deacon.

While Athanasius was a teenager, Emperor Constantine declared an end to the persecution of Christians. But all was not well in the church. A popular priest named Arius began teaching that Jesus was not coeternal with God the Father but was rather a divine creation. As Arius put it, "There was a time when the Son was not." Arius was a persuasive preacher and spread his ideas through poems and catchy songs. Arius's teaching convinced many, but other Christians were concerned that Arius's teaching conflicted with the faith for which the martyrs had died. Soon the church was embroiled in a controversy that threatened to upset the stability of the Roman Empire. Was the Son the eternal God, or was he a divine creation?

Constantine, concerned about the peace of his empire and wanting answers to this controversy, hosted a council in Nicaea. Church leaders from all over the known world were invited to attend. Deacon Athanasius's bishop had such confidence in his young deacon's grasp of trinitarian theology that he brought Athanasius with him to the council. Hundreds of Christians attended the council and, when the Arian controversy was put to a vote, all but two attendees affirmed the trinitarian faith. The council then drafted an early form of the Nicene Creed, a thorough summary of the apostolic trinitarian faith, as defined by Scripture.

In later decades, influential leaders in the Roman Empire and in the church turned against the theology of Nicaea. When Athanasius became bishop of Alexandria, his church was attacked and he was sent into exile five times for his belief in Nicene Christianity. Many told Athanasius that the entire world was against him. Athanasius replied that if the whole world was against the truth, "Then I am against the world!"[2] He became known as *Athanasius Contra Mundum* (Athanasius Against the World) for his stalwart defense of the faith.[3]

SCRIPTURE

"In the beginning was the Word, and the Word was with God, and the Word was God. He was in the beginning with God." (John 1:1-2)

MEDITATION: OF ONE BEING WITH THE FATHER

It's ironic that many seminaries offer courses with titles like Practical Theology, as if there were such a thing as Impractical Theology (Lord have mercy!). All good theology is practical. Of what practicality is the theology of Jesus being God the Son, second person of the Holy Trinity, coeternal with God the Father and God the Spirit?

Consider this: if Jesus were a created being, then a Christian could not enjoy the love, comfort, and compassion of a God who truly understands the human experience. Why? Because if Jesus were created, then he might individually and personally empathize and relate to the particular joys and pains of human existence, but God does not. God remains at a distance. Jesus came near, but God remained far. Jesus did the dirty work on the cross, but God kept his hands clean. Jesus gets us. God does not.

What kind of faith does this offer? A close, loving relationship with Jesus as semidivine teacher, friend, and leader, but a cold and distant relationship with God the eternal creator.

So when you pray, to whom are you praying? If it's to Jesus, then he might really want to help you out, but he lacks the power to do so. If it's to God, then he might have the power to help, but he lacks the love and compassion to do so.

The practical theology of the incarnation of the Son of God in the person of Jesus is absolutely essential to the integrity of the Christian faith and to a genuine experience of God's love. Because God has become a human being, we receive both the compassionate love and the divine power of God.

God understands *and* God is mighty to save.

God loves *and* God reigns.

Recite the Nicene Creed. Read *On the Incarnation* by Athanasius. Pray to the Father, through the Son, by the Spirit. Rejoice in the gloriously practical theologies of the Trinity and the incarnation.

PRAYER

Almighty and everlasting God, you have given to us your servants grace, by the confession of a true faith, to acknowledge the glory of the eternal Trinity, and in the power of your divine Majesty to worship the Unity: Inspired by the example of your servant Athanasius, keep us steadfast in this faith and worship, and bring us at last to see you in your one and eternal glory, O Father; who with the Son and the Holy Spirit live and reign, one God, forever and ever. Amen.[4]

THEOLOGIAN *(c. 1343–c. 1416)*

Commemoration: May 8
Time: Fourteenth and fifteenth centuries
Place: England

> *O God, of your goodness, give me yourself,*
> *for you are enough for me.*[1]

WHEN THE WORLD WAS CRUMBLING and death was all around, a faithful English woman named Julian reminded the church of the simple truth that God was loving and good and that "All shall be well." She lived in Norwich, England, during some of the darkest days of European history. In her lifetime, the deadliest pandemic in history, the Black Death, killed over 60 percent of the European population, somewhere between 75 million and 200 million people throughout Eurasia and Africa. In Julian's town of Norwich, half the city was killed by the plague, which persisted for most of Julian's life.

Julian fell ill at age thirty and experienced a series of visions so profound that she devoted the remainder of her life to contemplating them. She recorded these visions and contemplations in a book titled *Revelations of Divine Love*.

Understandably, during a period of so much death and societal collapse, much of the church was consumed with fear and dread, assuming that the plague was the result of God's wrath and a sign of the imminent end of the world. This makes Julian's writings all the more remarkable for her tender depictions of God and her confidence in his loving care. "By his might and will, he saves us and keeps us for love's sake," Julian wrote in her *Revelations*. "We will not be overcome by our enemy."[2]

In this time of terror and global chaos, the Lord moved Julian to observe a simple, small hazelnut as a microcosm of all of creation. "And he showed me . . . , a little thing, the size of a hazelnut, on the palm of my hand, round like a ball," Julian wrote. "I looked at it thoughtfully and wondered, 'What is this?' And the answer came, 'It is all that is made.' I marveled that it continued to exist . . . it was so small. And again my mind supplied the answer, 'It exists, both now and forever, because God loves it.' In short, everything owes its existence to the love of God . . . God made it . . . God loves it . . . God sustains it."[3]

Julian's writings of comfort and confidence in her loving God are the earliest known English-language writings by a female author. She lived in a small room on the side of the Norwich cathedral, keeping only a cat for company. She devoted her life to prayer and meditation and discipled those who sought her counsel, wisdom, and strength.

SCRIPTURE

"Anyone who does not love does not know God, because God is love."
(1 John 4:8)

MEDITATION: SUPERABUNDANCE

Why did God create the world? Was he lonely and wanted someone to talk to? Is he narcissistic and needs someone to worship him? Was he bored and wanted something to happen?

All of these unserious theories assume a kind of childish arbitrariness to God. But what if God were an emotionally mature adult? Why does a mature adult create anything? Is it not always out of simple love and pleasure in the thing?

A child may paint to please the parent. An adolescent may paint to prove something or to become famous. A mature adult likely paints because they love creating beautiful images with paint and brush. Mature creating flows from love.

God creates because he loves. He loves creating and he loves that which he has created. As priest/chef Robert Farrar Capon wrote,

> That, you know, is why the world exists at all. It remains outside the cosmic garbage can of nothingness, not because it is such a solemn necessity that nobody can get rid of it, but because it is the orange peel hung on God's chandelier, the wishbone in His kitchen closet. He likes it; therefore, it stays.[4]

This kind of loving pleasure we might call superabundance—an excess of love that overflows all containers. Chris Watkin explains,

> Neither we nor the universe are necessary. We may be important, precious, glorious even, but preciously and gloriously unnecessary.... In a theological register we might refer to it as grace, and we encounter this grace not first in redemption but in creation. It is through grace that the Christian is born again, but it is also through grace that the universe is born in the first place.[5]

This is not only the best way to understand the motives of God in bringing all of existence into being, but also the best way to understand the incarnation, life, passion, death, resurrection, ascension, and reign of Jesus. This is also the best way to understand the promises for the church at the end of the book of Revelation. The same superabundance of love that created the world ex nihilo also brought about the redemption of the world and will bring the world to its consummation.

It's love all the way through, from beginning to end. For this reason, Julian of Norwich was quite correct when she observed, "All shall be well, and all shall be well, and all manner of things shall be well."

Do you think of love as one minor aspect of God's character or as the core motive? If perceiving God's love for the world transformed Julian's experience of the monstrous tragedy of the Black Death, how might your perception of God's love transform your experience of your life right now?

A PRAYER OF JULIAN OF NORWICH

O God, of your goodness, give me yourself, for you are enough for me. I can ask for nothing less that is completely to your honor, and if I do ask anything less, I shall always be in want. Only in you I have all. Amen.[6]

MARTYRS OF SUDAN *(1983–Present)*

Commemoration: May 16
Time: Twentieth and twenty-first centuries
Place: Sudan

> *Hear the prayer of our souls in the wilderness.*
> *Hear the prayer of our bones in the wilderness. . . .*
> *Look upon us, O Creator who has made us.*[1]

TRADITION SAYS THAT CHRISTIANITY first reached Nubia (now Sudan) through the Ethiopian eunuch baptized by the deacon Philip (see Acts 8:26–40). The Christian faith grew deep roots in Nubia by the fourth century, and Nubia was ruled as a Christian kingdom for over a thousand years. Nubians developed a vibrant and distinctly African Christian culture until the sixteenth century, when Islamic empires conquered them. In the nineteenth century, Nubia was ruled by the British Empire.

Sudan gained independence in 1956 and experienced decades of war in subsequent years. In 1983, the government of Sudan declared an Islamic caliphate over the entire country. All citizens were ordered to convert to Islam or face extermination. On May 16, 1983, the Roman Catholic and Anglican Christians of South Sudan made a public, joint declaration that "they would not abandon God as they knew him."[2] The bishops, priests, and laypeople who signed this agreement knew that their signatures would almost certainly result in their deaths. Over the next decades, Christians suffered torture, death, and violence at the hands of jihadists. As in the early church, the blood of these martyrs has been the seed of the church in South Sudan, where Christianity has increased from 10 percent of the population in 1990 to 60.5 percent in 2020.[3]

In 2011, Sudan was divided into the northern Republic of Sudan, with an Islamic government, and South Sudan, with a Christian majority. But drawing boundaries on a map has not brought resolution to the crisis. Since 2003, between 80,000 and 400,000 people have been murdered in the Darfur region alone, in a mass slaughter now considered the first genocide of the twenty-first century. In the 2020s, the violence continued in Sudan, where Christians were caught in the crosshairs of a violent civil war between Islamist factions. It is estimated that today, over two million Sudanese refugees have fled to neighboring countries and almost ten million Sudanese citizens are internally displaced.[4] They are a stark reminder that the martyrdoms of the church are a present reality as the African church continues to rapidly expand in the twenty-first century.

SCRIPTURE

"As servants of God we commend ourselves in every way: by great endurance in afflictions, hardships, calamities, beatings, imprisonments, riots, labors, sleepless nights, hunger; by purity, knowledge, patience, kindness, the Holy Spirit, genuine love; by truthful speech and the power of God; with weapons of righteousness.... We have spoken freely to you, Corinthians; our heart is wide open. You are not restricted by us, but you are restricted in your own affections. In return (I speak as to children) widen your hearts also." (2 Corinthians 6:4-13)

MEDITATION: LIVING WITH AN OPEN HEART

How can we protect ourselves from getting hurt in the Christian life? How can we ensure that following Jesus will be good for our mental, emotional, and physical health?

These questions are normal for Westerners, but they are alien to the church in the majority of the world. Today, to live publicly as a Christian in Sudan requires a kind of vulnerability that many of us would deem unhealthy or dangerous. This kind of vulnerability is decidedly untherapeutic. But a faith that does not make sense of suffering is a faith that cannot deal with reality. It is an unreal faith. It is faith as a fantasy land that soothes your psyche but does not equip you to deal with cancer, betrayal, exile, or the firing squad.

Faced with antagonism to the Christian faith, most followers of Jesus will resort to one of three different postures: defensive, passive, or aggressive. Flight, freeze, or fight. Retreat from the culture, blend into society, or wage a culture war. Though these postures are natural (and we all have one of them as our default), they all stem from the same fear—fear of suffering. But are followers of a crucified Lord to fear suffering? Are we not to rejoice in our sufferings, knowing that suffering produces endurance, and endurance produces character, and character—hope, a hope that does not disappoint? Is not, then, suffering redemptive? As theologian Ed Clowney wrote, "Christ's suffering was redemptive not because suffering itself is redemptive, but because Christ himself is the Redeemer."[5]

One day I was driving to a retreat with some fellow church ministers, as we were talking and listening to each other's experiences of pain in ministry, we continually circled back to a version of that question, "How do you keep yourself from getting hurt in ministry?" We concluded, "You can't. You must live with an open heart." An open heart will be a wounded heart, perhaps even a broken heart. But sometimes the only way for a heart to be whole is for it to be broken.

What is your default posture toward society and culture: defensive, passive, or aggressive? Where is your heart closed? With the vulnerable courage of Christ, where might you widen your heart?

PRAYER

O God, whose arm is mighty to save, uphold, and deliver your servants in Sudan and all those who suffer for your name, bearing in their bodies the dying of our Lord Jesus, and as they have known the fellowship of his sufferings, make them to know the power of his resurrection, through the same Jesus Christ our Lord. Amen.[6]

DEACON AND ABBOT OF TOURS *(c. 735–804)*

Commemoration: May 20
Time: Eighth century
Place: Northumbria (now England) and Francia (now France)

*Men can be attracted but not forced to the faith.
You may drive people to baptism, [but] you won't
move them one step further in religion.*[1]

AS PAGAN EUROPEAN RULERS embraced Christianity during the church's first millennium, many kings and military leaders faced the temptation to impose their new faith through force. But coercion and Christian conversion are fundamentally incompatible, and Alcuin was one courageous Christian who spoke this truth to the power of his day.

Alcuin was born in eighth-century Northumbria and studied at the cathedral school in York. He was ordained a deacon and became such a well-respected scholar that his reputation spread throughout England and mainland Europe. Charlemagne, king of the Franks, invited Alcuin to serve as his adviser on religion and education. At the time, the Frankish kingdom was in the midst of one of the most infamous instances of systematic, forced conversions of pagans to Christianity. In decades past, Frankish kings had converted from paganism to Christianity. After decisively repelling invading Islamic armies, the Franks had taken up the mission of converting neighboring pagan warrior kingdoms to Christianity by adopting a policy of mass baptism, under the threat of death. This philosophy demonstrated a fundamental ignorance of Christianity and reflected the war practices of their non-Christian neighbors.

Alcuin carefully countered Charlemagne's policies, noting that people could not be forced into Christianity but should rather be "attracted" to the faith. The Frankish Christians, Alcuin said, should "be well-trained in the examples of the Apostles: let them be preachers not plunderers."[2] "New converts to the faith," Alcuin argued, "must be fed on gentler teaching as babies on milk. . . . Careful thought must also be given to the right method of preaching and baptizing, that the washing of the body in baptism be not made useless by lack in the soul of an understanding of the faith."[3] Baptism would have no effect, said Alcuin, if administered by violence.

Alcuin established schools and reforms that resulted in a flowering of art, science, literature, and philosophy in Charlemagne's kingdom. This bright period of cultural development was credited to Charlemagne and named the Carolingian Renaissance in his honor, but this rebirth of culture and learning could justly be named after Alcuin, who sowed the gospel of peace from which many blessings flowed.[4]

SCRIPTURE

"Oh, taste and see that the LORD is good!" (Psalm 34:8)

MEDITATION: THE SLOW WORK OF MISSIONAL PRESENCE

Ever tried to cook something too quickly, only to burn it? Some things simply cannot be rushed. As Pippin argued in *The Fellowship of the Ring*, "Short cuts make long delays."[5]

The conversion of unbelievers is one of these things. This is because a true follower of Jesus is an integrated person, someone whose inner and outer life are congruent. Forced conversions, whether coerced by Muslims or Christians or Hindus, are not effective. You can threaten a child with punishment to achieve obedience, but it will not win their heart (and will likely build resentment over time). You can force someone to eat a food, but you cannot force them to like it. For there to be genuine delight, there must be willing participation.

For this reason, the everyday missional labors of the church must be slow, patient, and gentle. The missional presence of the church must be one of warm hospitality, ever inviting outsiders to "taste and see that the LORD is good!" (Psalm 34:8). The invitations may be persistent, even to the point of irritation. But they must never stray into aggression or coercion. A true invitation contains no threats.

For the church to make the shift from thinking of missions as urgently and aggressively "taking ground" or "winning souls" to a more winsome invitation of love, there must be a shift from conceiving of missions narrowly as *action* to understanding missions more comprehensively as *presence*.

Action has a short timetable and is prone to focus on measurable results.

Presence, by its very nature, is focused more on the posture, tone, and long-term effect. Presence takes the long view.

Missional action is temporary—a short burst of activity, and then you need a break.

Missional presence can be permanent; it need not ever wear out.

Missional action tends to focus on enacting change.

Missional presence is focused on embodied virtue toward neighbors.

Missional action utilizes the neighbor for the sake of the church's good.

Missional presence utilizes the church for the sake of the neighbor's good.

As European Christendom was established and the bride of Christ frequently rejected her groom for tawdry affairs with political power, Alcuin was one of the voices that recalled the church to her first love. Today, we look on forced baptisms and can recognize the terrible harm that was inflicted. But I wonder, do we also recognize the places where Christians continue to seek coercive power today? For example, when a Christian is elected to a political position, whether to the head of the local school PTA or to the presidency of a nation, do we reckon with the temptation to pass legislation making unchristian behavior illegal? The second you have the power to force other people to behave in a particular way, you have the opportunity to make a missional shortcut.

Forced baptisms are a missional shortcut, but that particular shortcut is likely not available to you today. So rather than congratulating yourself for not participating in such abuse, it might be more profitable to wonder, what other shortcuts are tempting for you? Where do you need the patient, gentle love of Jesus for you to embody missional presence?

PRAYER

Almighty God, by your gift alone we come to wisdom and true understanding, and by your power you raised up your servant Alcuin to be a light of learning in his time. Look with favor, we pray, on our universities, colleges, and schools, that knowledge may be increased among us and wholesome learning flourish and abound. Bless those who teach and those who learn; and grant that in humility of heart they may ever look to you, the fountain of all wisdom, through Jesus Christ our Lord. Amen.[6]

VISIONARY *(c. 1412–1431)*

Commemoration: May 30
Time: Fifteenth century
Place: France

Go forward bravely. Fear nothing. Trust in God.[1]

WHEN THE FRENCH CRIED OUT TO GOD for deliverance from English oppressors, God raised up a humble peasant girl named Joan as his messenger. Joan lived in a farming region of northeast France during the Hundred Years' War. In this war, English nobility with ancient Norman/French ancestry fought with native French over land and property. The French peasants suffered many evils while the nobility fought over ancient claims. By the time Joan was thirteen, England had gained the upper hand in the war. God began speaking to Joan at this time through the voices of angels and saints. God was grieved by the injustice suffered by the French people and had heard their prayers. He gave Joan a daunting mission: she was to install an embattled Prince Charles as the next king of France and lead France to victory over their oppressors.

At age sixteen, Joan put on armor and journeyed eleven days to Charles's court. She told Charles that he was destined by God to be king and asked for an army that she would lead to liberate the city of Orléans. This bold, unprecedented act was bizarre to all at Charles's court. Charles's advisers said Joan was a delusional teenager. Charles ignored them and gave Joan an army. Riding a white horse, Joan led the French to victory over the English at Orléans, and Charles was crowned king. The tide of the war was turned.

Joan continued to receive visions and fight against English oppression. At age nineteen, she was captured by the English and condemned to death for witchcraft and heresy. As the flames consumed Joan's body, she issued her final words, calling on the name of Jesus. An English soldier said to those nearby, "God forgive us: we have burned a saint."[2] Twenty-five years after her death, a church investigation exonerated Joan of heresy. In 1920, the Roman Catholic Church officially recognized Joan of Arc as a saint.

SCRIPTURE

> "Let no one despise you for your youth, but set the believers an example in speech, in conduct, in love, in faith, in purity." (1 Timothy 4:12)

MEDITATION: TOO YOUNG TO BE USED BY GOD?

Joseph, Samuel, Ruth, David, Esther, Daniel, Mary, John, Paul, Timothy— what do they have in common? They were all "too young" for the work God called them to. The Lord calls and uses all types, young and old, men and women, rich and poor; but the too-young seem to have a special place of affection in his heart. The too-young person is obviously inadequate; they don't have enough life experience to be wise, and they rarely have enough resources to be effective. The too-young are, therefore, often the perfect kind of person for God to manifest his strength in weakness.

It is good common sense for local churches and denominations to have rules about how old someone must be in order to take certain steps: make a public profession of faith, be ordained for ministry, teach, lead, etc. But the church must also remember that she serves a Lord who loves to use the too-young and therefore must always be ready to make an exception to the general rules and regulations. You never know when you might have another Timothy or Joan of Arc on your hands!

What if Charles had listened to his advisers and dismissed Joan as the inexperienced teenager she was? What if Pharaoh had not listened to Joseph? What if Eli had not listened to Samuel? What if Samuel had not anointed David? What if Joseph (and Mary's parents!) had rejected her? What if the other disciples had rejected John (who was likely somewhere around fourteen years old when he became a disciple)? What if the early church had rejected Paul, and what if Paul had rejected Timothy?

What if you do not listen to the too-young people who are called by God in your life? What opportunity might you or your church miss if you are not open to God calling the too-young?

PRAYER

O almighty Lord, you were a strong tower to Joan of Arc and to all those who put their trust in you: Be now and evermore our defense. Look in pity upon all impacted by war, including the wounded and the prisoners, cheer the anxious, comfort the bereaved, succor the dying, and hasten the time when war shall cease in all the world, through Jesus Christ our Lord. Amen.[3]

TEACHER OF THE FAITH AND MARTYR *(c. 100–c. 165)*

Commemoration: June 1
Time: Second century
Place: Judaean Samaria (now West Bank)

*We used to hate and destroy one another and refused to associate
with people of another race or country. Now, because of Christ,
we live together with such people and pray for our enemies.[1]*

IN THE EARLY YEARS OF THE CHURCH, Christians were misunderstood by the Roman Empire as cultists, atheists (they wouldn't worship Roman gods), and insurrectionists. Justin applied his philosophical training to defend and clarify the Christian faith, seeking to end persecution. He was born to a Greek family in Samaria at the end of the apostolic age. Trained in Greek philosophy, Justin sought meaning in Plato and the Stoic philosophers but was left wanting more.

One day, while walking along the seashore, he noticed a mysterious old man following him at a distance. Striking up a conversation, the old man asserted that prophets far more ancient than the Greek philosophers spoke by the divine Spirit, foretelling the coming of God's son, the Savior Jesus Christ. The identity of this old man remains a mystery to this day. He was one of countless unknown saints that the Holy Spirit empowered to speak truth at the right time and place. Justin was compelled by the old man's testimony and embraced the Christian faith. Any truth found in the Greek philosophers, Justin concluded, existed only because it had been derived from the truth that is Jesus.

The death of Polycarp, bishop of Smyrna, compelled Justin to begin his vocation as a church apologist. Polycarp had been a mentor and shepherd to many. As a former disciple of the apostle John, Polycarp had served as a final living link to the age of the apostles. When Polycarp was publicly executed by the Roman Empire for refusing to deny his faith, Justin was deeply affected. He wrote a letter addressed to the emperor of Rome that sought to end the persecution of Christians. Justin defended the Christian religion and denounced the gods of Rome, elevating Christ as the true reconciler of all people. "We used to hate and destroy one another" but "now, because of Christ, we live together with such people and pray for our enemies."[2]

While defending the faith in this letter, Justin gave some of history's earliest surviving descriptions of Christian practices, including one of the earliest detailed descriptions of Christian Sunday worship. "On the day called Sunday," Justin wrote, "all who live in cities or in the country gather together to one place, and the memoirs of the apostles [New Testament readings] or the writings of the prophets [Old Testament readings] are read, as long as time permits; then, when the reader has ceased, the president verbally instructs, and exhorts to the imitation of these good things. Then we all rise together and pray . . . when our prayer is ended, bread and wine and water are brought, and the president in like manner offers prayers and thanksgivings, according to his ability, and the people assent, saying 'Amen.'"[3]

Over his lifetime, Justin utilized his philosophical training in logic and rhetoric to argue that Jesus was the divine *Logos* (a Greek philosophical concept used by the apostle John in John 1) and Savior of the world. His dialogues with Jews and pagans are some of the earliest apologetic works in Christian history. After decades of defending the faith, Justin was beheaded for refusing to sacrifice to the Roman gods.

SCRIPTURE

"For in Christ Jesus you are all sons of God, through faith. For as many of you as were baptized into Christ have put on Christ. There is neither Jew nor Greek, there is neither slave nor free, there is no male and female, for you are all one in Christ Jesus." (Galatians 3:26-28)

MEDITATION: KINGDOM DIVERSITY AND UNITY

Racism, xenophobia, and prejudice are not new sins or uniquely American or European sins; they are ancient evils that have corrupted individuals and societies since the fall in Genesis 3. When humanity rebelled against God, they also fractured the human race, dividing it against itself. Adam turns on Eve, Cain murders his brother and then fears that anyone who finds him will kill him, Noah endures violence from his neighbors— divisions that culminate at the tower of Babel, where language is confused and unity is broken. Ever since, our default view of the stranger is suspicion. We have even encoded this into what we call "good parenting," where we reinforce our children's natural fearfulness with phrases like "stranger danger."

But Christ, who is the new Adam, reconciles us not only to God, but also to each other. And he reconciles us not only to the "each others" that resemble us, but to the strangers. This is why the church is often at its best when it participates in the work of reconciling and reunifying strangers, enemies, and those who formerly despised each other. Christians are uniquely able to do this work because they have discovered that, in Jesus, the words of the apostle Paul in Galatians 3 are true. There may be ethnic, racial, cultural, and economic diversity, but in Jesus, there is no diversity of *value*.

Today, we take this for granted because a Christian social ethic lingers in Western society. We have retained the idea that men and women, brown and white, rich and poor, should be equal in freedom, dignity, and worth. But we have lost the underpinnings that support these convictions.

Justin was a second-century leader in establishing this new ethic of equality of value within groups of people with cultural and racial diversity. In this way, the church truly became a new kind of humanity, something the world had never seen before.

Though the Sunday morning hours of church services continue to be some of the most racially divided hours of the week, the way forward for the church is to look back toward the first centuries and recognize that unity with diversity is actually part of our heritage.

Does your fellowship with brothers and sisters in Christ reflect the kingdom diversity that has been made possible through unity in Jesus?

PRAYER

Almighty God, who raised up your servant Justin to proclaim your grace in the church, keep all your faithful people, that they may not be tempted away by any human conceit, nor avarice, nor worldly wisdom, but remain steadfast and immovable in the gospel of Jesus Christ, our only mediator and advocate. Amen.[4]

EVANGELIST AND TEACHER OF THE FAITH *(1889–c. 1929)*

Commemoration: June 19
Time: Nineteenth and twentieth centuries
Place: India, Pakistan, Afghanistan, Tibet

If we do not bear the cross of the Master, we will have to bear the cross of the world. . . . Which cross have you taken up?[1]

SUNDAR SINGH WAS A DEDICATED MISSIONARY who evangelized the East, living in simplicity as he shared the hope of the gospel. He was born to a Sikh family in northern India. As a child, he studied with a Hindu *sadhu* (an Indian holy man) and was taught from the Bhagavad Gita, one of Hinduism's religious texts. At the same time, Singh learned English at a local Christian school.

When Singh was fourteen, his mother died. In grief and anger, the young boy took a Bible and burned it page by page. He searched for meaning in religious devotion and theological questioning but was left in complete despair. On the brink of suicide, he offered up one final plea that the true God would reveal himself. In a dream, Jesus appeared to Singh. This singular event transformed the young man.

When Singh announced that he would become a Christian, he suffered abuse from his family and community. He was poisoned many times and had dangerous snakes thrown through his window. Nevertheless, he survived and was baptized at age sixteen.

Singh studied in Western seminaries but rejected the insistence that Western culture was necessary to spread the gospel. Much of Western thinking, he concluded, conflicted with the way of Jesus. He compared the hearts of many Westerners to a stone in a river, that had

> been lying a long time in the water, but the water had not penetrated the stone. It is just like that with the "Christian" people of the West. They have for centuries been surrounded by Christianity, entirely steeped in its blessings, but the Master's truth has not penetrated them. Christianity is not at fault; the reason lies rather in the hardness of their hearts. Materialism and intellectualism have made their hearts hard. So I am not surprised that many people in the West do not understand what Christianity really is.[2]

Singh undertook missionary journeys across India, Pakistan, and Afghanistan, dressed in the simple robe and turban of an Indian *sadhu* and wandering without possessions. Barefoot wherever he went, he was called the Apostle with Bloody Feet. His message was the simple gospel of Jesus. "There is a deep and natural craving in the human heart that can be satisfied nowhere except in God," Singh taught. "Most of us, suppressing our deepest longings and disdaining God, seek satisfaction from this world. Such a path can lead only to despair.[3] . . . Surely we shall find peace not by eliminating desire, but by finding its fulfillment and satisfaction in the One who created it."[4]

Singh was beaten and punished often for his teaching. His teaching and conduct remained peaceful, no matter how much abuse he received. "The true Christian's life is like sandalwood, which imparts its fragrance to the ax which cuts it without doing it any harm."[5] During a final missionary visit to Tibet, Singh disappeared while ascending a mountain in the Himalayas. His body was never recovered, and his disappearance and death remain a mystery.

SCRIPTURE

"But Jews came from Antioch and Iconium, and having persuaded the crowds, they stoned Paul and dragged him out of the city, supposing that he was dead. But when the disciples gathered about him, he rose up and entered the city, and on the next day he went on with Barnabas to Derbe." (Acts 14:19-20)

MEDITATION: MAMA DIDN'T RAISE A QUITTER

In your family of origin, when was it acceptable to quit something? Most of us have one set of rules for casual commitments (adult kickball, book club) and another for more serious commitments (work, marriage), but we all have a pain point that, if reached, will cause us to throw in the towel. What is your pain point when it comes to faith? How difficult would life have to be for you to walk away from Jesus?

The reality for most Christians is that we have a tendency toward self-deception when it comes to answering this question. "Oh, I would never abandon the faith!" we may say to ourselves as we skip Sunday worship in favor of brunch. Our problem is that we tend to believe we will be loyal in the big moments of testing while not even noticing that we have failed a small moment of testing. We tend to think of our loyalty to Jesus as something intangible that exists in our minds and hearts as opposed to something that we do with our bodies in space and time. It's the same problem that plagues the man who declares that he would never cheat on his wife, while he stays late at the office to chat with an attractive coworker and misses dinner at home.

When Sadhu Sundar Singh encountered Jesus, the transcendent beauty of Christ was something he could never quit. The apostle Paul had the same kind of encounter with Jesus and, like Singh, afterward he could never quit.

Both Singh and Paul had the experience of being beaten for their faith and left for dead. Both got up and went right back to work. If Marvel movies had been around at the time, they might have quoted Captain America in *The First Avenger*: "I can do this all day."

We practice this kind of gritty resilience in small moments of testing, where the path of least resistance leads away from Jesus. What small moments of testing are coming your way this week? How might you practice "no quit"?

PRAYER

Almighty and everlasting God, you called your servant Sundar Singh to preach the gospel to the people of India and the world: Raise up in this and every land evangelists and heralds of your kingdom, that your church may proclaim the unsearchable riches of our Savior Jesus Christ, who lives and reigns with you and the Holy Spirit, one God, now and forever. Amen.[6]

MONASTIC AND MARTYR *(330–405)*

Commemoration: July 2
Time: Fourth and fifth centuries
Place: Ethiopia and Egypt

You fast, but Satan does not eat. You labor fervently, but Satan never sleeps.
The only dimension with which you can outperform Satan
is by acquiring humility, for Satan has no humility.[1]

MOSES THE ETHIOPIAN (also known as "Moses the Black") is among the most prominent ancient desert fathers, cherished for his dedication to humility and peace. He was born in Ethiopia and joined a band of seventy-five violent outlaws in the Nile valley of Egypt. This band of thieves terrorized the local populace, and Moses, distinguished by his towering figure and violent nature, soon became the robbers' leader. While being pursued by the authorities, Moses hid in a monastery with Egyptian monks. There, he observed the peace of Christ through the witness and discipline of the monks. Moses repented of his violence and lawlessness, was baptized, and became a member of the monastery.

In his early years as a monk, Moses found it difficult to completely leave the habits of his old life behind. One day, Moses found several robbers stealing from the monastery. He overpowered them and dragged them to the chapel by force, where they too repented and became members of the monastic community.

Moses became frustrated with himself and with his lack of progress in attaining the holiness of life that he sought. His spiritual father, Isidore, invited Moses to join him on the monastery roof at dawn. Together they watched the sun creep to the horizon. "Only slowly do the rays of the sun drive away the night and usher in a new day,"[2] said Isidore to Moses. God was at work in Moses, slowly refining the once-violent outlaw into a powerful figure of peace and godly holiness.

In time, Moses became a respected monastic leader, known as Abba Moses (Father Moses), and many of his teachings were recorded and preserved. "If we took the trouble to see our sins we would not see the sins of a neighbor,"[3] Abba Moses taught. Abba Moses also said, "Do not be at enmity with anybody and do not foster enmity in your heart; do not hate one who is at enmity with his neighbor—and this is peace."[4]

When Abba Moses was an old man, violent raiders laid siege to his monastery. Moses forbade the monks from defending themselves but told them to flee for safety rather than take up weapons to fight. Abba Moses remained behind and was murdered by the bandits as he stood with his monastery in peace.

SCRIPTURE

"We ask you, brothers, to respect those who labor among you and are over you in the Lord and admonish you, and to esteem them very highly in love because of their work. Be at peace among yourselves. And we urge you, brothers, admonish the idle, encourage the faint-hearted, help the weak, be patient with them all. See that no one repays anyone evil for evil, but always seek to do good to one another and to everyone. Rejoice always, pray without ceasing, give thanks in all circumstances; for this is the will of God in Christ Jesus for you." (1 Thessalonians 5:12-18)

MEDITATION: THE RISE OF A NEW, URBAN MONASTICISM

The monastic movement emerged in the third century in response to the cultural decline of the Roman Empire and the need that many Christians were sensing for a new kind of dedication to holiness of life. This new movement would invite the participant into a life of submission, peace, discipline, community, virtue, love, labor, and prayer. The monastic movement saw itself as something of an antidote to the licentiousness of the empire.

While it is not possible to know whether contemporary Western society is truly in decline or merely experiencing a dip before another rise, it is true that many followers of Jesus today are sensing a renewed need to dedicate their whole selves to holiness in Jesus. For this reason, counterintuitive as it may seem to many, there is a renewed interest in monasticism among the younger generations. But the monastic impulse of today differs from its historic form in several key ways. First, it is noncloistered. Monastics do not withdraw from their cities; they are embedded within society. Second, its commitment is limited, not permanent. In our highly mobile society, monastics are free to come and go. Third, it is bivocational. Monastics usually hold some sort of part-time or full-time job in the marketplace.

If the new monasticism is embedded within cities, limited in commitment, and bivocational, then what makes it monastic? The answer is that the new, urban monasticism is a community of Christians who share a rule of life and who are seeking to help one another grow in Christlikeness.

What makes this different from a normal church? The honest answer would be, not much—except that most churches do not invite their congregants into this depth of spiritual formation.

Moses the Ethiopian, before his conversion, was about as unmonastic as a man can be. It is a testament to the power of sharing a rule of life within a community of believers that he was transformed from a violent outlaw into a man who peacefully gave his life away to violent outlaws. This kind of deep transformation is only possible through the Holy Spirit, and it requires community and personal discipline. These are the tools by which we partner with the Holy Spirit in our own transformation.

The new, urban monastic movement of our time is simply the latest form of seeking this partnership with the Spirit of Christ.

PRAYER

O God, your blessed Son became poor for our sake and chose the cross over the kingdoms of this world. Deliver us from an inordinate love of worldly things, that we, inspired by the devotion of your servant Moses, may seek you with singleness of heart, behold your glory by faith, and attain to the riches of your everlasting kingdom, where we shall be united with our Savior Jesus Christ, who lives and reigns with you and the Holy Spirit, one God, now and forever. Amen.[5]

MONASTIC LEADERS

"WHATEVER GOOD WORK YOU BEGIN TO DO, BEG OF GOD ...TO PERFECT IT."

"I ASKED MY LORD AND HE LISTENED TO ME."

Ora et Lab- ora

BENEDICT of NURSIA c.480–547 ‖ SCHOLASTICA c.480–543

BENEDICT, MONASTIC LEADER *(c. 480–c. 547)*
SCHOLASTICA, MONASTIC LEADER *(c. 480–c. 543)*

Commemoration: July 11
Time: Fifth and sixth centuries
Place: Italy

> *Whatever good work you begin to do, beg of God with most earnest prayer to perfect it.* **BENEDICT**[1]
>
> *I asked my Lord and he listened to me.* **SCHOLASTICA**[2]

BENEDICT LIVED DURING THE DECLINE of Roman civilization in Western Europe. He was troubled by the corruption and selfishness that plagued Rome as it crumbled into chaos. He left the comforts of society to fast and pray in a remote cave. His faith attracted others who wanted to join him. Soon Benedict began to consider how to organize monastic communities of monks to accommodate the many pilgrims. Taking inspiration from ancient African monastic principles, Benedict wrote an influential guidebook for establishing patterns of prayer and common labor, devoted to the good of the monastic community and society as a whole. "Relieve the lot of the poor," Benedict instructed, "clothe the naked, visit the sick, and bury the dead. Go to help the troubled and console the sorrowing. Your way of acting should be different from the world's way; the love of Christ must come before all else."[3] This guidebook became known as *The Rule of Saint Benedict* and it helped establish a mission for Benedictine communities that has survived for nearly fifteen hundred years. With his twin sister Scholastica, Benedict founded communities for men and women that transformed Western Europe through dedicated prayer, labor, and hospitality. The institutions (hospitals, schools, universities) and industry (arts, science, agriculture) cultivated in these monastic communities over the following centuries were fundamental to the rebirth of Western European civilization.

Benedict was known for his selflessness and resilient faith. With each small portion of dinner he received at his monastery, he would feed a morsel to a raven. This act of selflessness would save his life. When a disgruntled monk poisoned Benedict's bread, the raven grabbed the bread and flew out a nearby window.

Each year, Benedict made a special visit to his sister Scholastica's home, where they would fellowship and pray together. One year, at the close of day, Benedict insisted that he leave his sister's company. As prescribed by his *Rule*, men were not allowed to stay in women's quarters after dark. Scholastica knew that her dying hour drew near and she began to pray. Soon a violent storm broke out around her monastery. "Look," said Scholastica, "I asked you and you refused to listen to me. I asked my Lord and He heard me. Go now, if you can. Leave me behind and return to your monastery."[4] The author of the *Rule* was forced to acknowledge his sister's wisdom and remained with her while they enjoyed a final evening together.

SCRIPTURE

"Do not neglect to show hospitality to strangers, for thereby some have entertained angels unawares." (Hebrews 13:2)

MEDITATION: RESURRECTION ENTERTAINING AND CRUCIFORM HOSPITALITY

Today, entertaining guests and showing hospitality seem to be almost synonyms, but in reality they are nearly opposites. To entertain well these days is to put the skills and resources of the host on full display. The house is resplendent, the food is magnificent, the drinks are stunning, the clothes are breathtaking, the conversation is stimulating, the music is enthralling. To entertain well is to throw a killer party. When you leave a good party, you think, "Wow! That was amazing!" No shade thrown here—who doesn't love a good party? Parties can be a taste of the new creation, the marriage supper of the lamb.

But this is oh-so-different from hospitality. Hospitality is personal, intimate, quiet, vulnerable, and intrusive. Consider these words from the *Rule* of Benedict: "All guests who present themselves are to be welcomed as Christ. . . . By a bow of the head or by a complete prostration of the body, Christ is to be adored because he is indeed welcomed in them."[5]

If entertaining is more like resurrection, hospitality is more like crucifixion. (It's usually not quite that extreme.) The opportunity for hospitality is thrust on you when you're running late and are not prepared for guests. The opportunity for hospitality is with people you don't want in your house. The opportunity for hospitality is the chance to let yourself be interrupted the way Jesus was interrupted, the chance to let yourself be imposed on the way Jesus was imposed on.

Entertaining leaves you glowing. Hospitality leaves you tired and maybe just a bit frustrated.

Both are good, but in very different ways. The goodness of entertaining is obvious to us today. We love a cheery picture of attractive young people eating outside under string lights. But what is the goodness of hospitality? The goodness for the guest is self-evident. They receive shelter, succor, bread, and board. But is there goodness for the host?

The goodness of hospitality for the host is the solidarity they experience with Christ when they sacrifice their time, energy, and resources for the inconvenient good of another. There are some aspects of Jesus that can only be known when someone needs time you can't waste, money you can't afford, and room you don't have.

Benedict lived this cruciform hospitality and taught others to live it as well. If you love resurrection entertaining, where might you also open yourself to cruciform hospitality?

A PRAYER OF BENEDICT OF NURSIA

Gracious and holy Father, please give me intellect to understand you, reason to discern you, diligence to seek you, wisdom to find you, a spirit to know you, a heart to meditate upon you, ears to hear you, eyes to see you, a tongue to proclaim you, a way of life pleasing to you, patience to wait for you, and perseverance to look for you. Grant me a perfect end, your holy presence, a blessed resurrection, and life everlasting. Amen.[6]

OLGA, PATRON OF THE CHURCH IN RUSSIA AND UKRAINE *(c. 890–969)*

VLADIMIR, PATRON OF THE CHURCH IN RUSSIA AND UKRAINE *(c. 953–1015)*

Commemoration: July 15
Time: Ninth, tenth, and eleventh centuries
Place: Kievan Rus' (now Ukraine and Russia)

Through your prayers may I be preserved. OLGA[1]
I see light and I have seen Christ. VLADIMIR[2]

EVEN THE GREATEST SINNERS can be saved by our even greater Savior, and this is certainly evident in the story of the conversion of Olga of Kyiv. Olga was a merciless pagan ruler of the Kievan Rus'. When her husband was murdered while collecting tribute from the neighboring Drevlians, she vowed revenge. The Drevlians sent a delegation to Olga, proposing that she marry their prince to form a political alliance. Olga had the delegation buried alive in a mass grave. She burned a second delegation alive in a bath-house. She invited unsuspecting Drevlians to a funeral feast for her husband, and once they had drunk their fill of mead, she ordered a mass slaughter. She then promised the remaining Drevlian citizens peace if they would give her an offering of three pigeons and three sparrows from each household. The Drevlians dutifully obeyed, grateful that Olga's vengeance was over. It wasn't. Olga ordered her soldiers to tie burning, sulfur-soaked rags to each bird's foot and release the enormous flock, ablaze with fire. The terrified birds fled to their nests, consuming the Drevlians in flames. Fleeing Drevlians were captured by Olga's troops and either butchered or sold into slavery. No vengeance was enough for Olga. No injustice could be satisfied. No peace could be found, either in the land of the Rus' or within Olga's heart.

While on a diplomatic visit to Constantinople, Olga first encountered the Christian faith. The emperor of Constantinople proposed marriage to Olga, but Olga refused, saying that, as a pagan, she should not marry a Christian prince. The emperor arranged for Olga to receive the best Christian education directly from the archbishop of Constantinople, and she took to the teaching of the gospel like "a sponge absorbing water."[3] "Blessed art thou among the women of Rus'," the archbishop said to Olga, "for you have loved the light, and quit the darkness." Olga asked to be baptized, after which the delighted emperor proposed marriage. But Olga refused again. Her desire for the faith had not been a means for a political alliance. Olga sincerely wanted to bring the faith back to her native Rus'. She returned to her people and spent the remainder of her life praying for them and appealing to them to accept the gospel. Her grandson, Vladimir, remembering the witness of his grandmother, solidified Christianity as the faith of the Rus'. Olga's and Vladimir's conversions marked the establishment of the church in Ukraine and Russia.[4]

SCRIPTURE

"And you were dead in the trespasses and sins in which you once walked, following the course of this world, following the prince of the power of the air, the spirit that is now at work in the sons of disobedience—among whom we all once lived in the passions of our flesh, carrying out the desires of the body and the mind, and were by nature children of wrath, like the rest of mankind. But God, being rich in mercy, because of the great love with which he loved us, even when we were dead in our trespasses, made us alive together with Christ— by grace you have been saved." (Ephesians 2:1-5)

MEDITATION: METAMORPHOSIS

People do not change. This is the consistent testimony of psychologists, spouses, parents, best friends, and anyone who has lived long enough to be disillusioned of their romanticism. People might temporarily adopt new behaviors. They might try on a new personality like new clothes. They might pretend to change. But people do not change. Thus saith the realist.

And yet we have stories of people like the apostle Paul, who one minute was overseeing the stoning of Christians and the next was proclaiming Jesus as the way, the truth, and the life. We have stories of people like Olga of Kyiv, whose appetite for bloody vengeance was insatiable. That is, until she encountered the good news of the gospel. Then she became gentle, humble, prayerful, and oriented toward the good of others. These changes are so dramatic that there truly seems to be a wholly new and different person in place of the old.

Perhaps we might dignify and nuance the experience of many a weary therapist and say, "People cannot change themselves or each other, but God can change a person when they are willing to cooperate." An external power source is necessary for people to truly change, all the way down to the core of their personhood. The biblical image for this kind of change is just as dramatic as it feels when we witness it happen: they have passed over from death to life. The Bible is not shy or soft about describing our state apart from God's grace. We are dead. We are enemies. We are children of wrath.

When we think about Olga's life, this seems an apt description. But do we see the same insatiable pride and rage in ourselves? I do not have the opportunity or resources to destroy my enemies with impunity, but don't I set fire to their fields in my private imagination? Isn't there something inside you that just wants to go full-on scorched-earth on the people who have hurt you?

Olga discovered the love of God for her, despite her savagely violent heart, and it changed her. She didn't have to change in order to be loved; she was loved—and it enabled her to change. The same is true for you. You do not have to change in order to be loved; you are loved right now, as you are. Now, will you allow that love to change you?

PRAYER

Almighty God, by your Holy Spirit you have made us one with your saints in heaven and on earth. Grant that in our earthly pilgrimage we may always be supported by this fellowship of love and prayer, and know ourselves to be surrounded by their witness to your power and mercy; for the sake of Jesus Christ, in whom all our intercessions are acceptable through the Spirit, and who lives and reigns with you and the same Spirit, one God, forever and ever. Amen.[5]

NUN AND TEACHER OF THE FAITH *(c. 327–379)*

Commemoration: July 18
Time: Fourth century
Place: Cappadocia (now Turkey)

O Lord, you have freed us from the fear of death.
You have made the end of life here the beginning of a true life for us.[1]

MACRINA'S DEDICATION TO prayerful service was an inspiration for generations of Christians. She was the oldest of ten children of wealthy parents from Cappadocia, in the Roman province of Asia (now Turkey). She was named after her grandmother, Macrina the Elder, a revered Christian figure who had survived the fierce Roman persecutions of Emperor Diocletian. Macrina the Younger studied at the feet of her grandmother, and the young girl's faith and character began to resemble that of her elder, exhibiting a deep love for Scripture and theological study.

At age twelve, Macrina was betrothed to a rhetoric student. When the young man died before Macrina was old enough to marry, Macrina declared she would never marry anyone else. When her father died, Macrina resolved to remain with her mother and help manage the family's estate. Under Macrina's direction, the family's luxuries were renounced, and the family property was converted into a center for prayer and service to the poor. All the family's servants and slaves were given freedom and treated as equals.

Macrina gave a rich theological education to her younger siblings. Her brother Basil hoped to become a celebrated lawyer and left the family estate for higher education in Constantinople and Athens. When he returned home from school, he was "puffed up beyond measure with the pride of oratory."[2] Macrina confronted Basil's pride and convinced him to renounce his worldly ambitions and join her in a life of service to Christ. Basil came to embrace his sister's concern for the poor and would go on to become the bishop of Caesarea. Basil raised funds to build a large complex that housed an orphanage, a convalescent home, and one of history's first hospitals. This care facility, staffed by physicians and nurses, was unprecedented in its mission to provide care for people of all social ranks and classes.

Another of Macrina's brothers, Gregory, would become the bishop of Nyssa. He attributed much of his inspiration to the influence of his sister. Together with Basil, Gregory became one of the most significant defenders of the trinitarian doctrines of the Nicene Creed. Macrina encouraged Gregory as he faced hostility and temptation. Gregory of Nyssa honored his sister Macrina for her influence over their entire family. After her death, Gregory wrote a celebratory biography of his beloved sister that has become a classic of early Christian literature.

SCRIPTURE

"I am reminded of your sincere faith, a faith that dwelt first in your
grandmother Lois and your mother Eunice and now, I am sure, dwells
in you as well. For this reason I remind you to fan into flame the gift
of God, which is in you through the laying on of my hands, for God
gave us a spirit not of fear but of power and love and self-control."
(2 Timothy 1:5-7)

MEDITATION: FAITH AND FAMILY

Your immediate family members are often the most difficult people with
whom to grow in faith. Why is this? In our late-modern society, self-
actualization is (at least in part) defined as breaking away from the beliefs,
practices, and customs of your family of origin. Nobody needs to tell us this
directly; it's in the water. It is baked into societal expectations.

But this has not always been the case, and it does not necessarily have
to be the case for us today. In fact, one of the consistent themes of Paul's
Epistles is that after he finishes describing the way the gospel changes us,
he then continues with a section on family life—because family is the first
place we should learn to live out our faith.

Our family members know us in a way that nobody else does. Our family
members see the real us, not the carefully curated image we present to the
world. So many of us perform our faith like actors on stage, but we cannot
fool our family. Whatever faith we practice with family members, it must be
genuine, otherwise we will quickly (and accurately) be called out as a faker.

Macrina, Basil, and Gregory learned the faith from their grandmother
and from their parents. As they matured, they helped each other grow. They
challenged each other. They encouraged each other. It is no exaggeration
to say that the faith of this one family impacted the course of history.

Are you able to genuinely practice your faith around your parents,
grandparents, siblings, children, or grandchildren? If not, what holds you
back? Are you open to hear your family speaking into your experience
and practice of faith? Would you receive correction and guidance from
your family? Would you care enough to offer spiritual encouragement to
a family member?

Dear friend, you did not choose your family and they (likely) did not choose you. The Lord has given you to each other. Your family may not be the gift you want, but it is the gift you have! If practicing your faith with your family feels impossible, pray and ask for the Holy Spirit's help. The same God who placed you *in* your family will help you practice your faith *with* your family.

PRAYER

Almighty God, who has chosen your elect out of every nation and who shows forth your glory in their lives, grant, we pray, that, following the example of your servant Macrina, we may be fruitful in good works to the praise of your holy name, through Jesus Christ our Lord. Amen.[3]

MARTYR *(c. 289–c. 305)*

Commemoration: July 20
Time: Third and fourth centuries
Place: Antioch (Syria)

Lord, you have granted me to go through fire for your name.[1]

AT THE DAWN OF THE FOURTH CENTURY, Emperor Diocletian became alarmed by the rapid rise of Christianity. He believed this new faith was a cancer that weakened the empire and drastic measures were needed to uproot it once and for all. He rescinded Christians' legal rights and ordered the extermination of any Christian who would not offer worship to Rome's traditional gods. Margaret (also called Marina) is believed to have died during this persecution.

Margaret was a daughter of a pagan priest but converted to Christianity through the influence of a household servant. When she was fifteen, a Roman official discovered that she was a Christian and demanded she renounce Christ and become the official's property. She refused and was delivered to authorities for execution. She suffered imprisonment and cruel torments and was beheaded.

Later generations embellished Margaret's inspiring story of courage with fantastic details that unveiled the reality of the victory of Christ in Margaret's suffering. One account said that her tormentors set her on fire and the flames were miraculously quenched. Another account says that in the midst of her torment, she was swallowed whole by a demonic dragon and, through the power of the cross, burst the dragon into pieces from the inside.

SCRIPTURE

"For no one can lay a foundation other than that which is laid, which is Jesus Christ. Now if anyone builds on the foundation with gold, silver, precious stones, wood, hay, straw—each one's work will become manifest, for the Day will disclose it, because it will be revealed by fire, and the fire will test what sort of work each one has done. If the work that anyone has built on the foundation survives, he will receive a reward. If anyone's work is burned up, he will suffer loss, though he himself will be saved, but only as through fire. Do you not know that you are God's temple and that God's Spirit dwells in you? If anyone destroys God's temple, God will destroy him. For God's temple is holy, and you are that temple." (1 Corinthians 3:11-17)

MEDITATION: THROUGH THE FIRE

Fire is used physically and metaphorically all throughout the story of Scripture. Fire burns in the bush to draw Moses to hear God's voice, a pillar of fire lights the way for Israelites in the wilderness, fire consumes the water-soaked altar when Elijah prays, God describes himself as a consuming fire, tongues of fire rest on believers' heads at Pentecost, and a lake of fire is reserved for the devil and his ilk at the end of time. Everywhere fire appears in Scripture, a change is happening—calling, guiding, receiving, gifting, judging. Fire changes whatever it touches. Sometimes the change is for the better—when fire purifies. Sometimes the change is for the worse—when fire scorches.

Many of God's saints have faced the fires of persecution, and their physical bodies have been scorched and consumed. They have been judged by the world and damned to the fire. What has enabled so many men, women, and children to face the flames without fear? They were clinging to a promise—that their bodies would not only die, but also be raised up. As the apostle Paul said, "If anyone destroys God's temple, God will destroy him. For God's temple is holy, and you are that temple." While in Jerusalem, Jesus said the temple would be torn down and rebuilt in three days. His audience laughed, missing the metaphor. He was speaking of the temple of his own body. Christ's body was torn down in his flogging, his crucifixion, and his death. And his body was resurrected/rebuilt three days later.

The same promise of resurrection applies to all who now belong to him, and this is the promise that Margaret clung to when she faced the fire. This is why she did not say she was going *into* the fire, but going *through* it. She clung to the promise that there was a new life waiting for her on the other side.

What fire lies in front of you? How will you find the courage to walk through it? What awaits you on the other side?

PRAYER

Gracious Lord, who inspired the courageous witness of Margaret of Antioch, grant us not to be anxious about earthly things, but to love things heavenly; and even now, as we live among things that are passing away, to hold fast to those that shall endure, through Jesus Christ our Lord, who lives and reigns with you and the Holy Spirit forever and ever. Amen.[2]

COMPOSER *(1685–1750)*

Commemoration: July 28
Time: Seventeenth and eighteenth centuries
Place: Germany

I play the notes as they are written,
but it is God who makes the music.[1]

JOHANN SEBASTIAN BACH'S MUSIC has long been considered among the greatest artistic expressions in human history. When eminent scientist Lewis Thomas mused about what was the greatest testament of earth's achievements to send into deep space, he replied, "I would vote for Bach, all of Bach, streamed out into space, over and over again. We would be bragging, of course."[2]

In his lifetime, Bach was not one to brag. He lived a quiet life of hard work and dedication to his art, his faith, and his family. He received little recognition for his work in his lifetime, and he demanded little acclaim. Driven by a quiet, Lutheran piety, Bach worked as a church organist while he raised a large family and supplemented his income tutoring young students in music and Latin. He worked not for fame, but for God. Many of his music sheets were used as wastepaper after the performance. Of his one thousand known works, only 10 percent were published during Bach's lifetime. "I was obliged to work hard," Bach said. "Whoever is equally industrious will succeed just as well."[3] But Bach's compositions—such as the *Brandenburg Concertos*, the Cello Suites, the Mass in B Minor, and the *Goldberg Variations*—are evidence of a composer so profound that he shaped all subsequent Western music. Jazz musician Charles Mingus said, "Bach is how buildings got taller. It's how we got to the moon."[4]

Bach's music speaks of an inspiration that was dynamically tied to faith. Whether Bach was writing a profound religious work like the *St. Matthew Passion* or a comedic musical like the caffeine-laden *Coffee Cantata*, Bach considered all of his art for the glory of God. On his blank music sheets, Bach was known to write, "Help me, Jesus" and "In the name of Jesus." At the end of each finished composition, he would sign his works, *Soli Deo Gloria*—"Glory to God Alone."[5] Prayers and poems of praise were scribbled on Bach's manuscripts, revealing a joyful delight in his life and in his God. "On land, on sea, at home, abroad," Bach wrote, "I smoke my pipe and worship God."[6] This simple, joyful faith inspired the greatest music in history, music which continues to speak of the transcendent truths and joys of Christianity to such a profound degree that Bach has been nicknamed the Fifth Evangelist.

SCRIPTURE

"The LORD said to Moses, 'See, I have called by name Bezalel the son of Uri, son of Hur, of the tribe of Judah, and I have filled him with the Spirit of God, with ability and intelligence, with knowledge and all craftsmanship, to devise artistic designs, to work in gold, silver, and bronze, in cutting stones for setting, and in carving wood, to work in every craft. And behold, I have appointed with him Oholiab, the son of Ahisamach, of the tribe of Dan. And I have given to all able men ability, that they may make all that I have commanded you: the tent of meeting, and the ark of the testimony, and the mercy seat that is on it, and all the furnishings of the tent, the table and its utensils, and the pure lampstand with all its utensils, and the altar of incense, and the altar of burnt offering with all its utensils, and the basin and its stand, and the finely worked garments, the holy garments for Aaron the priest and the garments of his sons, for their service as priests, and the anointing oil and the fragrant incense for the Holy Place. According to all that I have commanded you, they shall do.'" (Exodus 31:1-11)

MEDITATION: COCREATING WITH GOD

God is the original artist. He speaks the universe into existence: spiraling galaxies, crystalline ice, erupting heat vents beneath the oceans, kingfishers in flight, ripening peaches, bellowing bison, hanging orchids, all pinnacling in the wonder of a human face. God is the master sculptor, composer, painter, scientist, gardener, rancher, chef, and architect. All the fearsome beauty of the natural world flows from his creative fingertips.

There are many rational arguments for the existence of God, but often the most compelling is the argument from aesthetic experience. We might frame it as a deductive argument: there is the music of Johann Sabastian Bach. Therefore there must be God.

Let that settle for a moment. This is the kind of argument that can only be accessed as the instinctive or gut level. As British philosopher Alain de Botton once quipped, "Although I don't believe in God, Bach's music shows me what a love of God must feel like."[7] His mind is not convinced, but his heart is wooed. This is what the beauty of God, his world, and the

God-like creativity of his image-bearers does to people. Every atheist must gaze out over the vastness of the Pacific or peer deep into the night sky or listen to Bach's Cello Suites and wonder if they've missed something.

When Christians think about the call to evangelism, we often think about using words to persuade the minds of unbelievers. This is good and right. But is it enough, I wonder? If there is a God who entices and woos his people with beauty, should not his people join his divine creativity as a testimony to his goodness?

The creative arts are not frivolous nonessentials; they are intrinsic to the *imago Dei*. When you create something good and beautiful, you are cocreating with God. You are also evangelizing. You are bearing witness to the existence of God.

PRAYER

O God, who inspired the worship of your servant Johann Sebastian Bach, who now delights to worship you in heaven, with saints and angels: be ever present with your servants on earth who seek through art and music to perfect the praises of your people. Grant them even now true glimpses of your beauty, and make them worthy at length to behold it unveiled forevermore, through Jesus Christ our Lord. Amen.[8]

OLAUDAH EQUIANO, RENEWER OF SOCIETY *(c. 1745–1797)*
WILLIAM WILBERFORCE, RENEWER OF SOCIETY *(1759–1833)*

Commemoration: July 30
Time: Eighteenth and nineteenth centuries
Place: Nigeria (Equiano) and England (Equiano and Wilberforce)

O you nominal Christians! Might not an African ask you—"Did you learn [the horrors of slavery] from your God who says, 'Do unto [others]?'" OLAUDAH EQUIANO[1]

Africa, Africa… Your sufferings no tongue can express. WILLIAM WILBERFORCE[2]

WILLIAM WILBERFORCE CHAMPIONED the abolition of the transatlantic slave trade as a member of the British Parliament. But Wilberforce's efforts would have been in vain without the grassroots labor of women and men like Olaudah Equiano, who appealed to the consciences and pocketbooks of their fellow countrymen.

Equiano was born in the kingdom of Benin (now Nigeria). He was captured as a child and sold into slavery in the Caribbean. He was sold twice more and experienced horrific conditions. In 1766, he purchased his freedom, and in the 1780s joined the Sons of Africa, an abolitionist movement in London. His bestselling autobiography, *The Interesting Narrative of the Life of Olaudah Equiano* (1789), vividly depicted the horrors of the slave trade and called polite English society to come to terms with the wickedness that it perpetuated. Equiano's autobiography also served as a spiritual narrative, detailing how he came to know Jesus and became active in the evangelical movement of the Anglican Church. Equiano's voice was a pivotal force that helped open the eyes of many to the truth about the horrors of the slave trade.

Equiano, Wilberforce, and many of their abolitionist colleagues were driven by the evangelical conviction of the first Great Awakening that called for the transformation of society according to the character of Jesus Christ. "So enormous, so dreadful, so irremediable did the [slave] trade's wickedness appear that my own mind was completely made up for abolition," Wilberforce said. "Let the consequences be what they would: I from this time determined that I would never rest until I had effected its abolition."[3] This great goal became a reality with the Slave Trade Act of 1807. Wilberforce also spearheaded efforts for global missions, the mass distribution of Bibles, the ethical treatment of animals, and many other reforms that we continue to strive to advance in modern society.

SCRIPTURE

"For if you keep silent at this time, relief and deliverance will rise for the Jews from another place, but you and your father's house will perish. And who knows whether you have not come to the kingdom for such a time as this?" (Esther 4:14)

MEDITATION: THE WORK THAT IS YOURS TO DO

Despite the omnipresent, omniscient, omnitemporal illusions that the internet and smartphones give to us, we cannot be everywhere, doing everything, all the time. You are always only in one place, at one time, doing one thing. Multitasking is a lovely myth, but in reality, it's just splitting our focus rather than working single-mindedly on one task at a time. When we do this, the quality of our work suffers.

If you are to resist the natural tendency to be mediocre at many things and instead do one thing with excellence, then you must face the limiting question, "What work is yours to do?" It's a question that nudges you to examine your sphere of influence. Where are you? When are you? What opportunities are available? What urgent needs might you address?

Frederick Buechner describes a vocation this way: "The place God calls you to is the place where your deep gladness and the world's deep hunger meet."[4] In order to do something well, you must start homing in, narrowing the scope, limiting the field to arrive at the work that is yours to do.

Both Wilberforce and Equiano burned with passion for justice to see the transatlantic slave trade end, and they had the position and the opportunity to enact change. How tragic it would have been if each had pursued different interests? How ineffective if they had pursued medicine, art, theater, music, architecture, and farming . . . all at the same time? There were so many other good labors to which they could have given *part* of themselves. Thank the good Lord they said a thousand *no*s to nearly everything else so that they could give a full-throated *yes* to one thing. Of course Wilberforce and Equiano worked on more than one project, but the common thread through all their life's work was justice and the renewal of society. They found their vocation. They knew what work was theirs to do, and they did it well.

Dear friend, what work is yours to do? What are all the places you need to say *no* so that you can give a robust *yes* to the one thing?

PRAYER

Almighty and eternal God, who empowered your servants Olaudah Equiano and William Wilberforce in their struggle against injustice and oppression, so fill our imaginations, so control our wills, that we may be wholly yours, utterly dedicated to you; and then use us, we pray, as you will, and always to your glory and the welfare of your people; through our Lord and Savior Jesus Christ. Amen.[5]

AUGUSTINE · BISHOP of HIPPO 354–430 & MONICA of HIPPO c.331–387

AUGUSTINE, BISHOP OF HIPPO (354–430)
MONICA, MOTHER OF AUGUSTINE (c. 331–387)

Commemoration: August 28
Time: Fourth and fifth centuries
Place: Thagaste and Hippo (now Algeria)

You have made us for yourself, O Lord, and our hearts
are restless until they rest in you. AUGUSTINE[1]

Nothing is far from God. MONICA[2]

MONICA WAS AN AFRICAN CHRISTIAN who watched her family slowly fall apart. Her husband cheated on her. Her son, Augustine, left the Christian faith for a decadent life in the big city. He became a slave to sexual addiction and the occult. For many years, Monica spent every night praying and weeping, pleading for the Lord to bring her son back into the truth.

The Lord kept every one of Monica's tears in his bottle (Psalm 56:8) and heard her prayers. Augustine's autobiographical *Confessions* beautifully recounts the many ways that God slowly and faithfully sought him and brought him to the truth. "O Lord, little by little with most tender and most merciful hand, touching and composing my heart, did you persuade me."[3]

One day, Augustine walked in despair in a garden when he heard a small child singing, "Take up and read." The nearest book was a collection of New Testament writings. Augustine opened it and read, "Let us walk properly as in the daytime, not in orgies and drunkenness, not in sexual immorality and sensuality, not in quarreling and jealousy. But put on the Lord Jesus Christ, and make no provision for the flesh, to gratify its desires" (Romans 13:13-14). "Instantly," Augustine wrote, "as I reached the end of this sentence, it was as if the light of peace was poured into my heart, and all the shades of doubt faded away."[4]

Augustine found himself immersed in the fullness of the faith, the fullness of beauty, and the fullness of joy in Jesus Christ that his mother had so long prayed he would receive. As a Christian, Augustine became a bishop and addressed many pastoral controversies, including confronting the cult of Manichaeism that had once had such a powerful hold on him. His greatest work, *The City of God*, is a cornerstone of Western theology. His writings have positioned him throughout history as the most influential theologian in all of Western Christianity.

SCRIPTURE

"Come to me, all who labor and are heavy laden, and I will give you rest." (Matthew 11:28)

MEDITATION: REST FOR THE WEARY

Are you tired? So many people today are wrapped up in the constricting coils of the two-headed snake: busyness and distraction. We are in such a hurry. Our to-do lists cannot fit into our calendars, and we live with a chronic sense of not enough. Not enough time. Not enough energy. Not enough resources.

Our hurried, busy schedules wear us out, and so we look for moments of relief and escape through distraction. We use technology, pharmaceuticals, caffeine, alcohol, and carbohydrates to give us a momentary dopamine boost before we plunge back into the chaos.

Where can our restless hearts, minds, and bodies find soul-restoring rest that we so desperately long to experience?

Jesus comes to us and says that what we are looking for, both in our busy work and in our faux-rest distraction, is him. Our exhaustion is a neon-lit billboard pointing to our need to collapse into the arms of Jesus. Only in Christ will we find the refreshment and restoration that our soul-weary selves so desperately need.

Why will we find this in Jesus? Because you and I were made to draw our life from God the way a tree draws its life from the soil and the sunshine. As Augustine observed, "You have made us for yourself, O Lord, and our hearts are restless until they rest in you."

Faith and baptism in Jesus reconnect us to God, the source of life. Once reconnected, the daily practices of silence, solitude, prayer, and Scripture reading (even if just for a few minutes) nurture this attachment to God.

Today, lay aside your busyness, resist the distractions of screens and snacks, help your body and mind to become quiet, and find your rest in Jesus.

A PRAYER INSPIRED BY THE WORDS OF AUGUSTINE

Heavenly Father, you have made us for yourself, and our hearts are restless until they rest in you. Look with compassion upon the heartfelt desires of your servants, and purify our disordered affections, that we may behold your eternal glory in the face of Christ Jesus, who lives and reigns with you and the Holy Spirit, one God, forever and ever. Amen.[5]

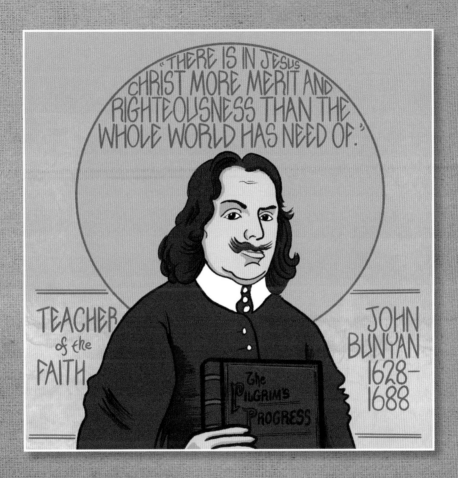

TEACHER OF THE FAITH *(1628–1688)*

Commemoration: August 30
Time: Seventeenth century
Place: England

*There is in Jesus Christ more merit and righteousness
than the whole world has need of.*[1]

JOHN BUNYAN, AN ENGLISH BAPTIST AND A PURITAN PREACHER, composed one of the most significant works of literature in the English language. He was born the son of a tinker and was largely self-educated. At age sixteen, he was drafted into the English Civil War, serving with Parliament's anti-royalist Republican Army. Bunyan would later confess that in his three years of conscription, "I was the very ringleader of all the Youth that kept me company, in all manner of vice and ungodliness."[2]

The Puritan army defeated the forces of King Charles I and established the Commonwealth of England, which governed England without a king, operating as a republic for over a decade, from 1649 to 1660. During this period, Bunyan married and had four children. His heart began to awaken to religious conviction, but his church attendance led him to despair. For years, he feared death and judgment and became convinced that he had somehow committed an unpardonable sin. He was overwhelmed by doubts, fears, and skepticism of the Christian faith. He searched the Scriptures for answers but remained troubled until, one day, a decisive moment occurred. "One day as I was passing into the field," Bunyan recounted, "this sentence fell upon my soul: Thy righteousness is in heaven. . . . I saw with the eyes of my soul Jesus Christ at God's right hand; there, I say, was my righteousness. . . . Now did my chains fall off my legs indeed."[3] From this moment on, Bunyan gained deep confidence in the limitless grace of Christ.

Bunyan committed himself to ministry and preaching but landed on the wrong side of political power. The English had grown tired of Puritan rule and reinstated a king in 1660. King Charles II wanted to stamp out noncon-forming insurrectionists and placed heavy restrictions on all ministers who refused to conform to the Church of England. Bunyan was arrested for holding a secret religious meeting and given a prison sentence of three months. When Bunyan refused to pledge that he would cease his noncon-formist preaching, this sentence turned into over twelve years in prison.

Many of Bunyan's greatest writings, including his famous book *The Pilgrim's Progress*, were composed from his prison cell. *The Pilgrim's Progress* is an allegorical fantasy story, depicting the harrowing adventure of the Christian pilgrim as he seeks to flee destruction and attain salvation in Christ's Celestial City. Along the way, he encounters giants, a demonic dragon, and many other characters who represent the realities of the

Christian life journey. *The Pilgrim's Progress* was published soon after Bunyan's release from prison and was an instant bestseller. Bunyan's plain language presented theological truths in a fashion that the great English writer Samuel Johnson later complimented, saying, "the most cultivated man cannot find anything to praise more highly, and the child knows nothing more amusing."[4] *The Pilgrim's Progress* remains one of literature's most translated and reprinted works in the English language.[5]

SCRIPTURE

"These all died in faith, not having received the things promised, but having seen them and greeted them from afar, and having acknowledged that they were strangers and exiles on the earth. For people who speak thus make it clear that they are seeking a homeland. If they had been thinking of that land from which they had gone out, they would have had opportunity to return. But as it is, they desire a better country, that is, a heavenly one. Therefore God is not ashamed to be called their God, for he has prepared for them a city." (Hebrews 11:13-16)

MEDITATION: LIFE AS A PILGRIMAGE

Where is home for you? You might think of the house where you spent your childhood, or perhaps the town where you grew up. Maybe you think of parents and siblings. Or do you think of the place you are now, a place you have chosen?

Some creatures have no need for a fixed home. Yellowfin tuna are not longing for a cozy cave to settle down with spouse and children. But humans are home-based creatures. Homelessness is one of the saddest and worst things that can happen to a human being, and a loving home, one of the best things.

And yet even those of us who have received that remarkable miracle of a loving home are not quite at home, are we? Maybe we picked the wrong city? Maybe the wrong neighborhood? The wrong house? The wrong spouse? Despite the glad tidings of our annual Christmas cards, we wonder ... why do I still not feel at home? Is there a home for me out there somewhere?

Jesus experienced this feeling and said, "Foxes have holes, and the birds of the air have nests, but the Son of Man has nowhere to lay his head" (Matthew 8:20). What does it say that even the Son of God felt homeless in this world? Does it not speak to the reality that humans are exiles, sojourners, pilgrims in this life?

One of the consistent metaphors for life used by the people of God, ever since Abraham left Ur of the Chaldeans, is that of a pilgrimage, a journey of faith through the wilderness toward the city of God. Christians of every age must identify their wilderness and conceive of their life as a long expedition toward their true home. Christians, like their Lord, are therefore never truly at home in this life. At best, all we get is a foretaste of that future homeland. John Bunyan knew this in his own life of faith, and he beautifully and creatively expounded on it in his *Pilgrim's Progress*. We hear it in the words of his main character, Christian, "I seek an incorruptible inheritance, undefiled, and one that fades not away, and it is laid up in heaven."[6]

Today, where are you feeling homeless? Where is there still some inner restlessness that longs to be at peace. Rather than misplace the blame on your house, family, job, neighborhood, or city, embrace the wilderness that is your life and continue to walk the pilgrim's way. You will not journey forever.

There will dawn a bright new day, your feet shall reach that distant shore, and we will say, with Jewel the unicorn, "I have come home at last! This is my real country! I belong here. This is the land I have been looking for all my life, though I never knew it till now."[7]

PRAYER

O God, for your servant John Bunyan and for all those who love you, you have prepared such good things as surpass our understanding. Pour into our hearts such love toward you, that we, loving you in all things and above all things, may obtain your promises, which exceed all that we can desire, through Jesus Christ our Lord, who lives and reigns with you and the Holy Spirit, one God, forever and ever. Amen.[8]

MARTYR OF PAPUA NEW GUINEA *(c. 1921–1942)*

Commemoration: September 2
Time: Twentieth century
Place: Papua New Guinea

I'll stay with the fathers and sisters.[1]

LUCIAN TAPIEDI WAS AMONG A GROUP of clergy, teachers, and medical missionaries ministering in Papua New Guinea in the 1930s and 1940s. The son of a Papuan sorcerer, Tapiedi came to faith in Christ at an Anglican mission school. He studied at St. Aidan's Teacher Training College and served as a teacher and evangelist. Tapiedi was known for his joyful spirit and love for learning, physical recreation, and music.

On January 4, 1942, the Japanese Empire launched an invasion of New Guinea as part of their offensive campaign across the Pacific. Philip Strong, Anglican bishop of New Guinea, instructed missionaries, evangelists, and clergy to remain at their posts, despite the extreme risks. "If we all left, it would take years for the church to recover from our betrayal of our trust. If we remain—and even if the worst came to the worst and we were all to perish in remaining—the church would not perish, for there would have been no breach of trust in its walls, but its foundations and structure would have received added strength for the future building by our faithfulness unto death."[2] Tapiedi and all of the bishop's staff chose to stay at their posts and suffer death, if necessary. With the Japanese invasion imminent, Tapiedi instructed his married colleagues, "Take your wives and families to the bush and hide. I am single. I'll stay with the fathers and sisters; it doesn't matter if the Japanese get me."[3] Tapiedi was among 333 Christians who were murdered during the Japanese invasion and occupation of New Guinea. Bishop Strong suffered bombings and machine-gunning and only narrowly escaped death himself.

After the war, Bishop Strong was criticized for refusing to order an evacuation of New Guinea. But the fruit of the martyrs' sacrifices resulted in a great renewal of the New Guinea church after the war. In 1947, Bishop Strong named September 2 as a commemoration of his fallen brothers and sisters, the Martyrs of Papua New Guinea. Today, Tapiedi's image is carved in limestone on the exterior of Westminster Abbey, honored among the twentieth-century's modern martyrs.

SCRIPTURE

"Only let each person lead the life that the Lord has assigned to him, and to which God has called him. This is my rule in all the churches. . . .

So, brothers, in whatever condition each was called, there let him remain with God." (1 Corinthians 7:17, 24)

MEDITATION: THE POWER OF STAYING PUT

When a monk joins a monastery, he or she takes a vow of stability, promising to live out the rest of their days in that place. The idea is that true spiritual formation in community can happen only when there is stability. If the members of the community keep rotating in and out, then the rhythms of work and rest, conflict and forgiveness, giving and receiving, leading and following, cannot knit a group of people together. If you have to keep replanting the tree, you'll never harvest any fruit.

So many of us experience fruitlessness in our Christian life because we keep replanting the tree, so to speak, as we move from neighborhood to neighborhood, city to city, in search of a better life. What we often do not realize is the affect that our leaving has on the people in the rearview mirror. How does our leaving affect those who are left? How does it affect the communities we leave behind?

To be fair, sometimes the leaving is good and necessary—a departure to care for a sick relative, or to serve an urgent need, or to proclaim the gospel to an unreached people. Then we commission our best to go forth with the Lord's blessing.

However, most leaving is of a different sort. We tend to leave because the grass is greener, the taxes lower, the housing cheaper, the jobs better, the people kinder. When Christians leave their neighborhood and city for a better life elsewhere, we tell a lie to the people we leave behind. We tell them that we were only there for what we could get out of it. We tell them that the Christian life is the same as any other life. When Christians leave, our absence speaks a word to our former cities, and it is a word of rejection.

If Christians are to embody the love to Jesus to our neighbors and city, then it must begin with simple presence, and presence requires stability. We might not make formal monastic-style vows, but we ought to be very resistant to uprooting.

It is a profoundly Christian thing to say of your neighborhood, "I hope they bury me here."

What would it take to uproot you from your place? How redemptively stubborn are you? How much grit do you have to stay when going is so much easier?

Lucian Tapiedi knew the value of stability. Even when staying became perilous, he did not budge. His refusal to abandon his place was the greatest testimony to the gospel that he could speak. He knew this because he knew that his Lord never gave up on his creation or his people. God is wonderfully stubborn in that way. Jesus just won't budge. Come hell or high water, he will not leave his people.

And so, as my friend Alan Briggs writes, "Stay forth!"[4]

PRAYER

O eternal Lord God, you hold all souls in life: Shed forth upon your whole Church in Paradise and on earth the bright beams of your light and heavenly comfort; and grant that we, encouraged by the good example of your holy martyr Lucian Tapiedi and all of those who have loved and served you, may enter with them into the fullness of your unending joy; through Jesus Christ our Lord. Amen.[5]

RENEWER OF SOCIETY *(1910–1997)*

Commemoration: September 5
Time: Twentieth century
Place: Macedonia and India

Find the sick, the suffering, and the lonely, right where you are—
in your own homes and in your families . . . in your workplaces and in
your schools. You can find Calcutta all over the world if you have eyes to see.[1]

MOTHER TERESA'S DEDICATION to the poor and suffering and her advocacy for human rights made her one of the most recognized humanitarians of the twentieth century. Born Anjezë Gonxhe Bojaxhiu, she was the youngest child of an Albanian family in Macedonia. As a young girl, she resolved to devote her life to service as a nun and missionary. At eighteen, she left to study at a Roman Catholic abbey in Dublin, Ireland, and was soon sent as a missionary to India, where she taught at St. Teresa's School in Darjeeling. Anjezë took the name Teresa as her own, upon taking her first religious vows.

Teresa moved to Calcutta in 1937 to work at a convent school, where she served as headmistress. She was struck to the heart by the miserable conditions of so many of her neighbors and friends in Calcutta. Malnutrition, violence, and disease wrecked the lives of millions. The school lacked teachers and food, and Teresa was forced to beg to feed her students. With her heart burdened, she became an Indian citizen and committed herself wholly to her fellow Indians. She founded the Missionaries of Charity in 1950 and abandoned her Western clothing, wearing instead a white and blue Indian sari for the rest of her life. Her organization grew to include over five thousand members in 133 countries and ministered to the poorest of the poor, managing homes for those suffering from tuberculosis, HIV/AIDS, and leprosy; and running soup kitchens, orphanages, schools, and many other ministries.

For much of her life, Teresa ministered in Calcutta, India, but later in life she occasionally left India to draw attention to humanitarian crises around the world. During the Lebanon War's siege of Beirut in 1982, Teresa joined a group of Red Cross workers to free thirty-seven children from a hospital. She ministered to those impacted by the famine of Ethiopia, the earthquake in Armenia, and the Chernobyl radiation. She became a global advocate for the preservation of all human life, including the unborn and those at the end of life. "By blood, I am Albanian," she said. "By citizenship, an Indian. By faith, I am a Catholic nun. As to my calling, I belong to the world. As to my heart, I belong entirely to the Heart of Jesus."[2]

SCRIPTURE

"'Lord, when did we see you hungry and feed you, or thirsty and give you drink? And when did we see you a stranger and welcome you, or naked and clothe you? And when did we see you sick or in prison and visit you?' And the King will answer them, 'Truly, I say to you, as you did it to one of the least of these my brothers, you did it to me.'"(Matthew 25:37-40)

MEDITATION: SEEING WITH EYES OF COMPASSION

Teresa already had a calling, a mission, and a ministry. She was busy doing very good things for the Lord and for others. Her selflessness was unquestionable. And yet she *still* had the eyes to see different needs, new needs, all around her. Rather than seeing all of these burdens as impediments to her work, she had the eyes to see them as *even more important* work.

Of all the remarkable things Teresa of Calcutta did, this may be the most unnoticed and uncelebrated. How often are you and I so focused on doing something—maybe even something for God—that we cannot see the needs and opportunities right in front of us?

It all comes down to our eyes. Do we have eyes to see?

In Christ's parable, the righteous ask, "Lord when did we *see* . . . ?" And he answers that they saw him when they saw the "least of these." In other words, when they had eyes of compassion to the needy around them, they had eyes to see God.

Sometimes the very thing that prevents me from seeing God is all of my activity for God. In the midst of my ministry in Bible studies, prayer groups, teaching, sermon writing, and counseling sessions, are my eyes open to see anything else that God might be doing? Is there a more important work to be done that perhaps is right in front of me?

What about you? When was the last time you slowed down long enough to widen your viewfinder to take in all of what is happening around you? Where are the real needs? Who is in crisis? Have you chosen to serve someone who doesn't really need your help over someone who is desperate for aid? Have you chosen to pursue someone far off and ignored the ones who are near?

One hallmark of Jesus' earthly ministry was his willingness to allow people in crisis to interrupt him. Jesus' schedule was full of activity and full of purpose. It wasn't like he didn't have important places to go or things to do. But he allowed interruptions because he saw with eyes of compassion.

The interrupting person was therefore not a nuisance or a barrier to the work; they *were* the work.

Pray that Christ give us his eyes of compassion, that we might see as he sees.

PRAYER

O Lord our heavenly Father, whose blessed Son came not to be served, but to serve, we ask that, just as you blessed Teresa of Calcutta, you would bless all who, following in Jesus' steps, give themselves to the service of others; endue them with wisdom, patience, and courage, that they may strengthen the weak, raise up those who fall, and being inspired by your love, worthily minister to the suffering, the friendless, and the needy; for the sake of him who laid down his life for us, your Son our Savior Jesus Christ. Amen.[3]

ABBESS OF BINGEN *(c. 1098–1179)*

Commemoration: September 17
Time: Twelfth century
Place: Palatinate of the Rhine (now Germany)

All of creation is a song of praise to God.[1]

HILDEGARD OF BINGEN WAS A PROLIFIC FIGURE, active throughout her long life as an influential church leader, theologian, mystic, visionary, poet, composer, and scientist. She was born the tenth child of a family in Germany, and her parents dedicated their daughter to the church. At age fourteen, she lived in a small room with a religious hermit named Jutta, who was six years her senior. Jutta became a confidant and mentor to Hildegard, and it was with Jutta that Hildegard shared one of her greatest secrets—that since a very young age, Hildegard had been receiving divine visions from heaven.

Hildegard kept this secret very private until, at the age of forty-two, she received a vision in which God unveiled understanding and wisdom about creation and the spiritual life. "The heavens were opened and a blinding light of exceptional brilliance flowed through my entire brain. And so it kindled my whole heart and breast like a flame, not burning but warming."[2] The vision instructed Hildegard to begin writing down what God had told her over the course of her life.

Hildegard began writing down all that had been revealed to her over a lifetime of visions. Her writings were extensive and covered a wide range of subjects, including botany, medicine, theology, and music. Her musical compositions are considered one of the origins of Western classical music. Hildegard believed that making music brought one closer to God. "Words symbolize the humanity of the son of God," Hildegard wrote, "but music symbolizes his divinity."[3] Hildegard collected her musical compositions into a large compendium, which she called the *Symphonic Harmony of Celestial Revelations*.

Hildegard is also considered the founder of scientific natural history. Her writings on medicine were widely respected, and many journeyed to seek her healing skills in using plants and herbs. She taught that because all of creation was made by God, all plants and animals had unique purposes and uses for humankind. She believed that scientific study was a critical component of the church's holistic life.

Hildegard's reputation for wisdom made her a prominent leader in medieval Germany, and she was called on to resolve disputes among clergy. Today, she is among a short list of historical theologians officially bestowed with the title doctor of the church.

SCRIPTURE

"O LORD, our Lord,
　　how majestic is your name in all the earth!
You have set your glory above the heavens.
　　Out of the mouth of babies and infants,
you have established strength because of your foes,
　　to still the enemy and the avenger.

When I look at your heavens, the work of your fingers,
　　the moon and the stars, which you have set in place,
what is man that you are mindful of him,
　　and the son of man that you care for him?

Yet you have made him a little lower than the heavenly beings
　　and crowned him with glory and honor.
You have given him dominion over the works of your hands;
　　you have put all things under his feet,
all sheep and oxen,
　　and also the beasts of the field,
the birds of the heavens, and the fish of the sea,
　　whatever passes along the paths of the seas.

O LORD, our Lord,
　　how majestic is your name in all the earth!" (Psalm 8)

MEDITATION: EVERYDAY MAJESTY

When one of my daughters was barely a year old, she heard rain falling outside. It seemed a strange, unusual sound to her. She crawled to a window, pulled herself up, and peered out at the wondrous mystery: water was *falling* from the sky. She turned her head toward my wife and gestured toward the window with wide eyes that seemed to say, "Mama, can you believe what is happening out there?" My wife walked over and knelt beside her; cheek to cheek, they stayed for several moments, looking and wondering together.

When I returned home from work that evening and heard from my wife about our daughter's discovery of rain, it struck both of us as a tremendous gift to see the world through her eyes for a few moments. To us, rain is a boring, inconvenient, almost everyday kind of thing. But as my wife explained to our child, "We need water to live, and it just falls right out of the sky onto us. It's quite amazing."

We are surrounded by the glory and majesty of the natural world, but many of us have become so accustomed to it that we no longer notice it. It's like the year I rented an apartment close to train tracks: the first few weeks, the roar of a passing train was deafening; but after a few months, I could not hear it anymore. Only if someone new visited my place and commented with something like, "How can you stand all that noise?" would I notice that a train was passing.

Hildegard was blessed with vision. She not only had eyes to see the spiritual visions that God gave her, but also eyes to see the natural world for the glorious, majestic wonder that it is. When people encountered Hildegard, they began to see the world through her eyes. Her vision opened other people's eyes to the majesty of God in the created order.

Do you have eyes to see, or has the majesty of God's nature become boring to you? Who might help you to see?

PRAYER

Almighty God, who inspired your servant Hildegard of Bingen as she looked to you and who blessed her work with abundant fruit: your loving hand has given us all that we possess. Grant us grace that we may honor you with our substance, and, remembering the account which we must one day give, may be faithful stewards of your bounty, through Jesus Christ our Lord. Amen.[4]

PRIEST AND MARTYR OF KOREA *(1821–1846)*

Commemoration: September 20
Time: Nineteenth century
Place: Korea

No matter how fiercely the powers of this world oppress and oppose the church, they will never bring it down.[1]

CHRISTIANITY WAS INTRODUCED TO KOREA in the late eighteenth century by Korean laypeople who encountered the faith while studying in China.[2] The kingdom of Korea had been isolated from the outside world for many centuries by rulers who were suspicious of foreign influences. Despite this isolation, many Koreans were compelled by the teachings of Jesus, and a grassroots movement soon became widespread in Korea long before outside churches could provide clergy or institutional infrastructure. Many Confucian Koreans were hostile to the new faith, and thousands of converts were put to death for refusing to offer incense to their ancestors.

Among these martyrs was the first ordained Korean priest, Andrew Kim Taegon. Kim's father had been martyred when Kim was young. Kim was bolstered in his faith, despite the dangers, and determined to seek theological education and ordination. This meant leaving Korea while still a teenager to study the faith in China and the Philippines. After nine years of education, he was ordained in Shanghai and returned to Korea as the first Korean-born Christian priest.

Kim's ministry did not last long. At age twenty-five, he was executed near Seoul. In his final exhortation before he was beheaded, he encouraged his flock, "No matter how fiercely the powers of this world oppress and oppose the church, they will never bring it down. Ever since his ascension and from the time of the apostles to the present, the Lord Jesus has made his church grow even in the midst of tribulations. For the last fifty or sixty years, ever since the coming of the Church to our own land of Korea, the faithful have suffered persecution over and over again. . . . But, as the Scriptures say, God numbers the very hairs of our head and in his all-embracing providence he has care over us all. . . . Hold fast, then, to the will of God and with all your heart fight the good fight under the leadership of Jesus."[3]

SCRIPTURE

"And I tell you, you are Peter, and on this rock I will build my church, and the gates of hell shall not prevail against it." (Matthew 16:18)

MEDITATION: COURAGE, DEAR HEART

The apostle Peter often waffled between moments of incredible courage and crushing insecurity. He walked on water, was the first to confess that Jesus was the Christ, and swung his sword to defend his rabbi from arrest. He also sank with doubt into that same water and denied knowing Jesus when confronted. Peter was ready to follow a triumphant King, but he was not ready to follow a failed leader.

It is not surprising that Jesus directed these words to Simon when he renamed him Peter and prophesied that the church would persevere to the end. Peter would need this promise, and so do we. There have been many times where the gates of hell have indeed appeared to prevail against the church. Persecutions do not always lead to revivals; sometimes they effectively stamp out the faith.

When Kim was executed, his life and ministry on this earth were finished. In the battle between Kim and Confucianism, he lost. Confucianism won.

Therefore it is vital for Christians to recognize the difference between the eschatological nature of Christ's promise and the present, temporal weakness of the church.

Jesus did not promise that your local congregation would thrive. Jesus did not promise that your denomination would grow. Jesus did not promise that the church would endure in your specific nation-state.

Rather, the promise of the triumphant church is the promise of the future wedding supper of the lamb, where the bride of Christ and the bridegroom consummate their love and dwell together in eternal peace within the restored heavens and earth of the new creation.

Until then . . .

Christians will suffer and many will abandon the faith. Local congregations will close. Seminaries will shut their doors. Church buildings will be repurposed as high-end apartments. Denominations will fold.

All will seem to be lost, and the enemies of God will dance on the graves of the fools who clung to the name of Jesus.

The story of the church will appear to have come to an end and the book will close.

And yet. *And yet . . .*

The gates of hell will not prevail. The trumpet will sound, and the dead in Christ will rise first. The light shines in the darkness, and the darkness has not (nor will it ever) overcome it.

Kim lost the battle, but he will win the war. And so will all who trust the words of Jesus.

Fear not, Peter. Fear not, friend. Courage, dear heart.[4]

PRAYER

Let your continual mercy, O Lord, cleanse and defend your church in Korea and throughout the world; and because your church cannot continue in safety without your help, protect and govern it always by your goodness, though Jesus Christ our Lord, who lives and reigns with you and the Holy Spirit, one God, forever and ever. Amen.[5]

FRIAR, DEACON, AND REFORMER
OF THE CHURCH *(c. 1182–1226)*

Commemoration: October 4
Time: Twelfth and thirteenth centuries
Place: Italy

Where there is love and wisdom, there is neither fear nor ignorance.
Where there is patience and humility, there is neither anger nor vexation.[1]

IN AN AGE WHEN THE WESTERN CHURCH was embroiled in military conflict and political intrigue, Francis of Assisi was called to remind Christians of the peace and humility of Christ. As a young man, Francis enjoyed
music, parties, fine clothes, rich food, and wealthy friends. But over time,
he became disillusioned and began to ask if there was more to life than
luxury and comfort. He swore off his possessions and became a poor
beggar, praying that Jesus would reveal himself. One day, while praying in
an old church, Francis heard Jesus speak to him. "Francis, go and repair
my house which you see falling into ruin."[2] At first, Francis took this re-
quest literally. Slowly and painfully, Francis labored to rebuild the old
church building by hand.

But while Francis was repairing the building, Jesus was building in
Francis a deep love for the poor. Francis began feeding lepers and
preaching to the poor, and his ministry soon attracted disciples. He
founded a monastic order devoted to simplicity and poverty that imitated
the life of Jesus. Members of the Franciscan order gave up personal possessions and traveled throughout the world, preaching the good news of
the gospel of peace.

Francis believed all of creation reflected God's glory and was made
good, but that it groaned because of human sin and eagerly awaited
Christ's return. Francis proclaimed hope not only to all people, but also
to animals—proclaiming the good news of the new creation in Christ.
Francis ministered to the sick, the outcasts, and enemies. During the
Fifth Crusade, he traveled with a small company of unarmed brothers
and preached the gospel to the Egyptian Sultan al-Kamil. Because of
Francis's charity and grace, Islamic rulers gave concessions to the Franciscans. The Franciscans were allowed to serve as the custodians of
Christian holy sites in Jerusalem. Today, members of Franciscan orders
can be found around the world, in Roman Catholic, Anglican, and Lutheran traditions.

SCRIPTURE

"Blessed are the meek, for they shall inherit the earth." (Matthew 5:5)

MEDITATION: THE STRENGTH OF GENTLENESS

Meekness is not considered a desirable virtue for most inhabitants of Western cultures. This is especially, though not exclusively, true for men. It is a great misfortune that the New Testament Greek word *praeis* is translated into an English word that rhymes with weak. But meekness is not weakness; it is better understood as strength under control, exercising power while avoiding harshness. Meekness has far more in common with discipline and self-control than it has with being delicate or frail. Meekness is not a condition that life thrusts on you. Meekness is something you may choose, cultivate, and practice. If you desire to, you can become more meek over time.

Why will the meek inherit the earth? One theologian joked that the reason the meek inherit the earth is that they are the only ones left after all the aggressive folk have killed each other off. But the meaning is deeper. Jesus spoke this beatitude to Jews living in their promised land while it was being occupied by the Roman Empire. His word to them is, you do not need to raise up an army to take back your land; God will give it to the meek. The meek will inherit the earth because they are the ones who live in a posture of humble reception. They do not take; they receive—and so they will inherit.

Jesus was many things, but he was not weak. Imagine the strength and courage of Jesus to go willingly to the whipping post, to the cross, to the grave. Meekness is a word to describe the gentle strength of Jesus, the strength that, through gentleness, overcame sin and death. This gentle strength is planted within every Christian who calls on the name of Jesus and receives his Spirit into their being. If the meekness of Christ now dwells within you, in seed form, will you cultivate it, nurture it, help it grow? Will you practice Christlike meekness?

Francis lived a life of aggressive hedonism in his youth. Only after Jesus spoke to him did he become the gentle yet strong leader we remember today.

Do you desire to grow in meekness? Where might you exercise the gentle strength of Jesus today?

A PRAYER IN THE TRADITION OF FRANCIS OF ASSISI

Lord, make me an instrument of your peace. Where there is hatred, let me sow love; where there is injury, pardon; where there is discord, union; where there is error, truth; where there is doubt, faith; where there is despair, hope; where there is darkness, light; where there is sadness, joy. O divine Master, grant that I may seek not so much to be consoled as to console, to be understood as to understand, to be loved as to love. For it is in giving that we receive, it is in pardoning that we are pardoned, and it is in dying that we are born to eternal life. Amen.[3]

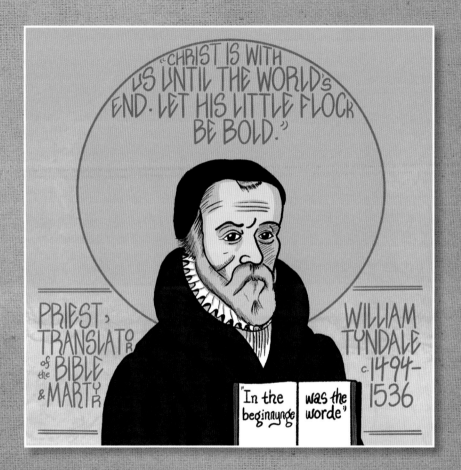

PRIEST, TRANSLATOR OF THE BIBLE,
AND MARTYR *(c. 1494–1536)*

Commemoration: October 6
Time: Sixteenth century
Place: England

Christ is with us until the world's end. Let his little flock be bold.[1]

WILLIAM TYNDALE WAS AN ENGLISH PRIEST and early admirer of Martin Luther's teaching. Tyndale had a deep desire to see every man, woman, and child in England given the opportunity to read Scripture in their native language. Earlier generations had prohibited the translation and reading of the English Bible, except with special permission. This prohibition had been an attempt to control the spread of false interpretations and false teaching. Only clergy and academics were authorized to read and interpret Scripture. Tyndale believed that this policy needed to change. He translated the New Testament and much of the Old Testament into English, in opposition to the restrictions of the Church of Rome and the restrictions of King Henry VIII's newly independent Church of England. Henry VIII's wrath was kindled even more when Tyndale openly criticized the king's desire to annul his marriage to Catherine so that the king could marry Anne Boleyn. Tyndale argued that Henry VIII's annulment and remarriage were in rebellion to God's Word. Tyndale fled to mainland Europe, anticipating Henry VIII's imminent order for his arrest. But agents of the king betrayed Tyndale into the hands of rulers in the Holy Roman Empire, and he was tried and condemned for heresy. Before his execution, Tyndale's last words were, "Lord! Open the King of England's eyes!"[2]

The Lord answered Tyndale's final plea. Within four years, multiple English-language Bibles were officially approved for distribution by Henry VIII, all based on Tyndale's work. Tyndale's translation was influential in nearly all subsequent English Bible translations. Many famous biblical phrases demonstrate Tyndale's masterful language skills, including, "In him we live and move and have our being" (Acts 17:28), "Fight the good fight" (1 Timothy 6:12), and "The spirit is willing, but the flesh is weak" (Mark 14:38). Most English translations today, like the King James Version and the English Standard Version, demonstrate Tyndale's monumental influence.

SCRIPTURE

"These words that I command you today shall be on your heart. You shall teach them diligently to your children, and shall talk of them when you sit in your house, and when you walk by the way, and when you lie down, and when you rise. You shall bind them as a sign on your hand, and they shall be as frontlets between your eyes. You shall write them on the doorposts of your house and on your gates." (Deuteronomy 6:6-9)

MEDITATION: PEOPLE OF THE BOOK

God's people have always been formed by the Word of God. The world was created by the Word; humanity was formed by the Word, commissioned by the true Word, and led astray by a false word; the Israelites were marked by the Word of the law; Christ is the Word made flesh, and thus we are redeemed by the Word. Now the church is the people who seek to embody the Word to a lost and weary world that knows only harsh and empty words. And so there are few artifacts in existence more vital than the Bible, God's Word written.

Followers of Jesus today are to read, study, memorize, contemplate, obey, and delight in the Word of God. For this, many forms of engagement are necessary. We need expository preaching, nuanced classroom teaching, inductive studies, lectio divina, reading of long passages of Scripture in public worship, and personal, devotional Bible reading. While many of us may take this last practice for granted, we must remember that for much of church history, the Bible only existed in Latin, Greek, Hebrew, and Aramaic. If your native language was a local dialect of, say, English, French, Italian, Spanish, Swahili, German, Chinese, or Cherokee, then you only had two avenues to access Scripture. You could attend a university and learn the ancient languages, or you could attend a local parish and hope that your priest would take the time to verbally translate the Scriptures from the Latin Vulgate into your native tongue.

Unfortunately for millions of Christians, they did not have the resources for the first, nor the good fortune of the second. And thus, biblical illiteracy was not merely a discipleship problem, it was the norm.

The convergence of the invention of the printing press and the scholarly labors of William Tyndale and others produced, for many, the first Bible that could be read by the average English-speaking person. This led to an explosion, not only of biblical understanding, but also of literacy in general.

When you hold in your hand a Bible written in your native language, you hold a treasure that few Christians throughout history have possessed. Cherish it. Read it. Memorize it. Meditate on it. We have always been people of the Word. What a gift that, in our time, we are also people of the Book.

PRAYER

O God, our heavenly Father, who raised up your faithful servant William Tyndale to be a pastor in your church and to feed your flock, give abundantly to all pastors the gifts of your Holy Spirit, that they may minister in your household as true servants of Christ and stewards of your divine mysteries, through Jesus Christ our Lord, who lives and reigns with you and the Holy Spirit, one God, forever and ever. Amen.[3]

MISSIONARY AND MARTYR *(1929–1960)*

Commemoration: October 14
Time: Twentieth century
Place: Pakistan

Leave all other ties. Jesus is calling.[1]

ESTHER JOHN WAS A COMMITTED Christian convert and missionary. She was born into an Islamic family in Pakistan and named Qamar Zia. While attending school, Zia was influenced by the Christian faith of her teacher and was inspired to study the Bible. Isaiah 53, in particular, was instrumental in her conversion to Christianity. In this chapter, the Old Testament prophet Isaiah spoke of the coming Messiah as a suffering servant: "Surely he has borne our griefs and carried our sorrows. . . . He was crushed for our iniquities; upon him was the chastisement that brought us peace, and with his wounds we are healed" (Isaiah 53:4-5).

Zia's Christian faith and her Bible study remained a secret for years, and she feared that she would be forced into an Islamic marriage. In her early twenties, Zia ran away from home and journeyed to Karachi, where she worked in a Christian orphanage and changed her name to Esther John.

Esther John worked in a mission hospital and later attended a Bible training school in northern Pakistan, where she lived with Presbyterian missionaries. As an evangelist, she traveled from village to village on a bicycle, teaching women to read and working alongside them in cotton fields. Her faith touched the lives of many. Some were led to Christ; others were hostile to the gospel and to Esther John. Eventually, her evangelism led to her martyrdom. In 1960, at age thirty, she was found murdered in her bed. But her murderer could not silence her message. Her name has become an emblem of Christian martyrdom in Pakistan. In 1998, in memory of this courageous missionary, a statue of Esther John was placed above the west door of Westminster Abbey, alongside nine other modern martyrs of the Christian faith.

SCRIPTURE

"Truly, I say to you, no prophet is acceptable in his hometown." (Luke 4:24)

MEDITATION: TO YOUR OWN PEOPLE

It would have been so much easier for Zia to leave Pakistan and become a missionary to a different group of people, perhaps those without an Islamic heritage. In a different setting, Zia would have been celebrated as a hero and her ministry welcomed as a gift. Instead, she ministered to her own people, people with the same background, same language, same culture. This gave her a significant missional advantage over those who travel to do missions in faraway places. Zia was a native; she understood the context from the inside. However, it also gave her a costly disadvantage.

Nobody likes a hometown prophet.

Hometown prophets represent a rejection of the hometown way of life. Their very presence rubs people the wrong way. This isn't the way we do things. This isn't how we brought you up. Who do you think you are to judge us, to call us to change? We know who you are. You're nothing special. Where did you get these wild ideas? Calm down and let's get back to business as usual.

When Jesus observed that prophets are not accepted in their hometown, it was not a call for his followers to go do missions work somewhere far away. It was a revealing statement that showed what his missional presence would cost him—his life.

Esther John experienced the same dynamic, and her life was taken right around the same age that Jesus' was.

Who are your people? What language, culture, context, and network of relationships is native to you? Let that be the first place you embody the missional presence of Jesus, before you contemplate a call to some faraway place.

PRAYER

Lord Jesus, you commanded us to make disciples of all nations, and you inspired the mission of your servant Esther John to the people of Pakistan. Bless all those who work together for the spread of the gospel; make them faithful and true witnesses to proclaim your glorious name. Send down the grace of the Holy Spirit upon all your people, that we may give cheerfully of our substance for the evangelization of the world, and that the light of your truth may shine brightly in every place. Hear us, O merciful Savior, who with the Father and the Holy Spirit lives and reigns, one God, world without end. Amen.[2]

TEACHER OF THE FAITH *(1515–1582)*

Commemoration: October 15
Time: Sixteenth century
Place: Spain

---

*All things pass; God never changes. Patience attains all that it strives for.
He who has God finds he lacks nothing. God alone suffices.*[1]

TERESA OF ÁVILA WAS A SPANISH NUN OF JEWISH ANCESTRY. She was an author, mystic, and religious reformer. Her mother died when Teresa was young. Her father was a strict man who imposed harsh discipline on his daughter. As a young girl, she was motivated by a deep faith, but in her early teen years, she became more enamored of friends, fashion, and reading adventure stories. She felt profound guilt for this, likely because of the austere presence of her father. At sixteen, her father sent her to a convent school, but instead of reinforcing her father's guilt-laden ideology, the school reignited Teresa's faith. After a year-long illness, Teresa emerged with refreshed vision for her service to God. Every saint was once a great sinner, Teresa concluded. Therefore, no matter how great her faults, even she could be part of God's family. At this time she began to experience rapturous visions of the burning, all-consuming love of God. These visions served as inspiration for her life's work.

Freed from the shackles of shame, Teresa became a devoted spiritual director to many, advising her colleagues in prayer and contemplation. She became known for her good humor, sharp wit, and love of life.

After years as a nun in a Carmelite convent, Teresa became increasingly concerned that the Carmelites had grown too inattentive to prayer and service and too concerned with wealth and status. She established a convent of her own, and in time, it would influence reform in the entire Carmelite order. Teresa faced opposition from many in Roman Catholic leadership who preferred the status quo. A legate of the pope described her as a "restless wanderer, disobedient, and stubborn femina."[2] Despite this opposition, she produced a large library of writings on spirituality and theology. She wrote many influential works, including a classic of personal examination, *The Interior Castle*. In this book, Teresa compared the human soul to a castle with seven layers of inner chambers. The deeper pursuit of God was charted by entering the inner regions of the soul through stages of prayer and contemplation. Teresa's teachings became a hallmark of Christian spiritual direction.

Forty years after her death, Teresa was declared a saint by the Roman Catholic Church. In the twentieth century, she was named one of the first female doctors of the church, an exclusive, small list of particularly influential saints posthumously recognized for their influence on theology and doctrine.

SCRIPTURE

"Let him kiss me with the kisses of his mouth! For your love is better than wine; your anointing oils are fragrant; your name is oil poured out; therefore virgins love you. Draw me after you; let us run. The king has brought me into his chambers." (Song of Solomon 1:2-4)

MEDITATION: THE BRIDE OF CHRIST

The Bible makes use of many metaphors to describe the relationship between God and his people. We are sheep, and he is our shepherd. We are chicks, and he is the mother hen. We are branches, and he is the vine. We are soil, and he is a farmer. We are his children, and he is our father. We are stones, and he is the builder. We are the clay, and he is the potter.

One of the most important (but least understood) metaphors used in Scripture is that of marriage, with the church as bride and Jesus as groom. Why least understood? Because this may very well be the most intimate of all metaphors, and intimacy can make some of us uncomfortable. Marriage is the most intimate human relationship—two people becoming one flesh. Sexual consummation is the fullest expression of covenantal commitment that humans are capable of making; and the fruit of that consummation, children, is the birthing of new life, a new creation.

Many people relate to God as father, teacher, savior, ruler, king, provider, comforter, counselor, and friend. But have you *experienced* relating to him as lover? That word experience is a crucial one. Intellectually contemplating God as lover is one thing; experiencing intimacy with God in this way is quite another. Consider the difference between reading a textbook of human anatomy and walking into the honeymoon suite with your new spouse!

Teresa had a vague knowledge of God in her mind through theological instruction in her childhood. But her faith ignited when she was enraptured by the ecstasy of knowing God as lover.

Just as a marriage is consummated after the wedding by the sexual union of husband and wife, so our faith will one day be consummated when we sit down at the table to celebrate the marriage supper of the lamb. Then we will fully realize that we are the long-lost love of Jesus the groom, and the empty ache in our hearts will be soothed by the lover we have been looking for all our lives.

PRAYER

O God, by your grace your servant Teresa of Ávila, kindled by the flame of your love, became a burning and shining light in your church, turning pride into humility and error into truth. Grant that we may be set aflame with the same spirit of love and discipline, and walk before you as children of light, through Jesus Christ our Lord, who lives and reigns with you, in the unity of the Holy Spirit, one God, now and forever. Amen.[3]

FRIAR *(1579–1639)*

Commemoration: November 3
Time: Sixteenth and seventeenth centuries
Place: Peru

Everything—even sweeping, scraping vegetables, weeding a garden, and waiting on the sick—could be a prayer, if offered to God.[1]

IN COLONIAL SOUTH AMERICA, Martin of Porres graciously served with humility and love in the midst of insults and prejudice. He was born in Lima, Peru, the illegitimate son of a Spanish father and a mother of African and native Panamanian descent. The culture of the day placed a stigma on Martin's mixed race and illegitimate birth, and Martin bore this burden his entire life. His father abandoned the family when Martin was young, and his mother was forced to work as a launderer. Throughout a childhood of poverty, mistreatment, and desperation, Martin fostered a vibrant prayer life and compassion for the poor and hopeless.

At age twelve, Martin began an apprenticeship with a barber/surgeon. At the time, the same person who cut hair also performed surgeries and prescribed medicines. Martin soon began a ministry to the sick. His colleagues witnessed him praying late into the night, often in ecstatic conversation with Jesus.

At fifteen, Martin tried to join a Dominican monastic order in Lima, but Peruvian law prohibited full membership for descendants of Africans or Native Americans. Martin stayed with the monastery as a servant, cleaning, doing laundry and kitchen work, and ministering to the sick. After nine years of service, his gentleness and healing hands earned the respect of the head of the monastery, Prior Juan de Lorenzana. De Lorenzana ignored the discriminatory Peruvian laws and allowed Martin to take vows as a full member of the community. Martin was assigned to manage the monastery's infirmary, and he continued in this position for the rest of his life. His humility, gentleness, medical skill, and love were a testament to his faith. He served all who were in need, whether they were of European, African, or native Peruvian ancestry. He was even known to offer his healing skills to domesticated and wild animals. This radical and countercultural love gained admirers among many, including wealthy donors who entrusted Martin with the finances necessary to found Lima's first orphanage and a hospital for abandoned children.

SCRIPTURE

"Now when the sun was setting, all those who had any who were sick with various diseases brought them to him, and he laid his hands on every one of them and healed them." (Luke 4:40)

MEDITATION: THE HANDS OF THE KING ARE THE HANDS OF A HEALER

As the saying goes, *"A healthy person has a thousand wishes; a sick person, only one."* All of us who are, or have ever been, seriously ill know this is true. Most days I struggle to even remember to pray. But when the flu hits and I lie on the bathroom floor in the middle of the night shaking with fever and covered in cold sweat, I am ready to talk with God! Then comes the bargaining, negotiating, and extravagant promising. *O Lord, I will do whatever you want if only you will heal me!* In hindsight, these desperate prayers are a bit funny and embarrassing. They are forgotten so quickly once health returns. Of course, the humor evaporates if the illness is terminal or the injury life threatening.

Our bodies are so very frail, aren't they? It doesn't take much for them to falter, crash, and die. The grass withers, and the flowers fade.

God made our bodies and called them good, and they continue to bear his goodness. For this reason, though our bodies are corrupted by sin and doomed to die, God has not abandoned our bodies. His hands are the hands of the Great Physician. Sometimes, in this life, he touches us and heals us. When this happens, we experience a miracle and behold his healing power. Other times he works through doctors, nurses, physical therapists, pharmacists, and other health care providers. Their healing hands are an embodiment of the King's hands, whether they know it or not.

Christ worked through Martin's hands to heal men, women, and children; young and old; livestock and wild creatures. The healing they experienced from Martin was but a foretaste of the great healing that is in store for all who come to Jesus for care. As the hors d'oeuvres precede the entrée, so medical care in this life precedes the resurrection of the body in the life to come. The dead will rise, and our bodies be raised incorruptible. Hallelujah!

Until that day, join the long labors of Martin and all others who have used their hands to care for the sick and injured bodies of those in need.

PRAYER

Almighty God, whose blessed Son Jesus Christ went about doing good, and healing all manner of sickness and disease among the people, and who gave

Martin of Porres gifts of healing and peace: Continue Jesus' gracious, healing work among us; console and heal the sick; grant to all physicians, nurses, and assisting staff wisdom and skill, diligence and patience; prosper their work, O Lord, and send down your blessing upon all who serve the suffering; through Jesus Christ our Lord. Amen.[2]

MONK AND MISSIONARY *(c. 1756–1837)*

Commemoration: November 15
Time: Eighteenth and nineteenth centuries
Place: Russia and Russian Alaska (now United States)

From this day, from this hour, from this minute we shall strive to love God above all else and to fulfill his holy will.[1]

HERMAN WAS A RUSSIAN ORTHODOX MONK who arrived with a cadre of brothers as a missionary to Kodiak in the Russian colony of Alaska in 1794. At the time, Russian Alaska was in the midst of a "fur rush," where Russian frontiersmen harvested pelts and furs and sold them to European and Chinese customers. Herman was shocked by the Russians' harsh treatment of indigenous Alaskans and the rampant alcoholism and corruption of the Russian settlers. The Russians forced Native Americans to hunt seals in the bitterest weather, and women and children were subjected to abuse and exploitation.

Herman and his fellow monks quickly became the defenders and benefactors of the native people and fierce critics of the corrupt Russian fur company that subjected native Alaskans to cruel conditions. He was attacked by Russian business leaders as a hack and a busybody. The monks were denied provisions promised by the Russian company and were forced to grow their own food. But Herman was deeply loved by the indigenous Alaskan people for his gentle, pastoral care. It's estimated that Herman baptized over seven thousand native Alaskans in the Kodiak region.

As an old man, Herman desired to spend his remaining years in solitude and moved to isolated Spruce Island, where he lived in a small cabin in the forest. He was visited so frequently by native Aleuts that, in time, Herman built a chapel, a guesthouse, and a school to accommodate the many pilgrims.

SCRIPTURE

"One day, when Moses had grown up, he went out to his people and looked on their burdens, and he saw and Egyptian beating a Hebrew, one of his people. He looked this way and that, and seeing no one, he struck down the Egyptian and hid him in the sand." (Exodus 2:11-12)

MEDITATION: CHOOSING A PEOPLE TO DEFEND

Did Moses identify as an Egyptian or an Israelite? He could have chosen the Egyptian identity. Raised in Pharaoh's court by royalty, Moses had access to every economic and political privilege. But Moses embraced his Israelite identity, he hated the oppression of his people by the Egyptians, and he resolved to do something about it. Tragically, he took vengeance into his own hands. Not only was this a great evil, but it was also ineffective. Not even the Israelites thought the murder by Moses accomplished anything. It took forty years of exile as a shepherd in Midian before Moses was ready to listen to God and to seek justice for his people God's way.

Like Moses, Herman faced a similar identity decision when he arrived in Alaska. Would he identify as a Russian and exercise his privilege, or would he identify with the native Aleuts and seek justice for them? Like Moses, Herman chose to identify with the oppressed, which made him a traitor in the eyes of the Russians. Herman was bad for business. But unlike Moses, Herman did not take vengeance into his own hands. He did not strike out in violence, but rather labored quietly, patiently, and gently for the good of the native peoples.

In a culture where many people try on new identities like new clothes, with whom will you choose to identify? Will you choose an identity that give you advantages, privileges, and opportunities for advancement? Or will you choose to join the cause of the poor and the oppressed?

Let's say you're a middle-class person who moves into an economically diverse neighborhood. Do you adopt the priorities and causes of your wealthy neighbors or your impoverished neighbors? At the local city council meeting, do you vote for a park to be developed into high-end apartments and stores, which will increase neighborhood property value? Or do you vote to keep the park because the local elementary school is already under-resourced and won't be able to accommodate the influx of new families if population density increases? Will you identify with the advantaged or disadvantaged?

Christ became a human being, and he surely would have had an easier life he had become incarnate as a Roman prince rather than a Jewish carpenter. The way of Jesus is the way of Moses is the way of Herman. Will it be your way?

PRAYER

O God, who inspired the mission of Herman to the people of Alaska, you have made of one blood all the peoples of the earth, and sent your blessed Son to preach peace to those who are far off and to those who are near: Grant that people everywhere may seek after you and find you; bring the nations into your fold; pour out your Spirit upon all flesh; and hasten the coming of your kingdom; through Jesus Christ our Lord. Amen.[2]

"SERVE GOD OBEDIENTLY WHEN IN HEALTH, AND RENDER THANKS TO HIM FAITHFULLY WHEN IN TROUBLE OR BODILY WEARNESS."

ABBESS

HILDA of WHITBY c·614–680

ABBESS *(c. 614–680)*

Commemoration: November 19
Time: Seventh century
Place: Northumbria (now England)

Serve God obediently when in health, and render thanks to Him faithfully when in trouble or bodily weakness.[1]

HILDA WAS BORN INTO A ROYAL HOUSEHOLD in Northumbria, now England. Her family was caught in the turmoil of her day. Her father was poisoned by a neighboring king, and her kingdom was invaded by pagans from Mercia. A monastic leader, Aidan of Lindisfarne, challenged Christians to devote themselves to a monastic life of prayer and fasting, and Hilda answered this call and became a nun. Her wisdom and administrative skills were valued by the church, and she became the leader of a significant Celtic abbey in Whitby, serving as abbess for a community of women and men. She oversaw the community's spiritual life and managed the abbey's farming, animal husbandry, and woodcutting.

In the midst of her responsibilities, Hilda took time to minister to the individual needs of those in her care. In one famous instance, she became aware of a herdsman named Cædmon who sang beautiful songs of praise. She urged Cædmon to write more songs and poems and saw to it that his skill was encouraged through education and the community of the monastery. Today, Cædmon's lyrics are among the earliest poetic writings in Old English and he is the earliest English poet whose name is still remembered today. His talent may well have been lost to history were it not for the encouragement of Hilda. The ancient English historian Bede recounted, "All who knew her called her mother because of her outstanding devotion and grace."[2]

Mother Hilda's wisdom was consulted for pivotal governing decisions. Kings, princes, and church officials sought her insights and sought her help to resolve disputes. In 664, the church in England struggled to decide whether to keep ancient Celtic worship practices or become united with the Roman-style worship of Western Europe. The synod of Whitby met to discuss this question at Hilda's abbey, with Hilda present at the council. Out of a desire for church unity, the synod opted to submit to Roman customs. The church in England would remain part of the Roman Catholic Church for the next 870 years.

In her later years, Hilda suffered from a debilitating illness, and her hard work, courage, and faithfulness amid her suffering was a powerful witness. She governed her monastery through her illness and founded a new monastic community in her final year of life.

SCRIPTURE

"O Jerusalem, Jerusalem, the city that kills the prophets and stones those who are sent to it! How often would I have gathered your children together as a hen gathers her brood under her wings, and you were not willing!" (Matthew 23:37)

MEDITATION: YOU NEVER STOP NEEDING MOM

The work of a mother is often dismissed, demeaned, discouraged, and degraded. If you ask a woman what she does for a living and she replies, "I'm a homemaker," she will likely receive a pitying look and a patronizing, "Well, good for you."

All societies are built on a foundation of mothers. This takes nothing away from the essentiality of fatherhood. I (Marotta) am one myself, and I know my presence with my kids is crucial to their development and well-being. But as one of my sons said to his brother when I was packing up to leave for an overnight work trip, and the brother wailed that I could not go because he *needed* me to stay with him: "It's going to be okay, we don't *neeeeeed* Dad."

Ouch. The kid knows he needs his Mama, and on that point, he's right.

Even as we grow, mature, and become adults, we never stop needing our mothers—because good mothers are an embodiment of the true motherhood of God, the source of our life. We never stop needing God, and so likewise we never stop needing Mom. (If your mother has passed or if you are estranged from her, you likely know this better than the rest of us. You know the pain of absence.)

Hilda became a spiritual mother to hundreds and hundreds of homeless souls who were longing for the sheltering parenthood of God and found a taste of it under her roof. What might that tell us about the need for spiritual mothers today? Christians can argue about gender roles in church leadership until the end of the world, but we can all agree that everyone needs both biological and spiritual mothers. We need wise, experienced, strong women to bring the mothering presence of Christ to bear on the souls of their spiritual children.

Sisters, have you embraced the call to spiritual motherhood? Brothers and sisters alike, who are the spiritual mothers in your local church? Do you perceive your need for them? What gratitude and dignity have you shown them?

PRAYER

O God, without whose beauty and goodness our souls are unfed, without whose truth our reason withers, just as you consecrated the life of Hilda of Whitby, so consecrate our lives to your will, giving us such purity of heart, such depth of faith, and such steadfastness of purpose, that in time we may come to think your own thoughts after you, through Jesus Christ our Savior. Amen.[3]

TEACHER OF THE FAITH *(1898–1963)*

Commemoration: November 29
Time: Twentieth century
Place: Northern Ireland and England

*Next to the blessed sacrament itself, your neighbor
is the holiest object presented to your senses.*[1]

CLIVE STAPLES (C. S.) LEWIS WAS AN OXFORD SCHOLAR who expanded
the imaginations of many readers with insightful and profound writings.
He grew up a member of the Anglican Church of Ireland, but by age fifteen,
he identified as an atheist. He said that for much of his young adulthood,
he was conflicted in his atheism. He was "very angry at God for not existing"
and "equally angry with him for creating a world."[2] As a young man, he
served in World War I in France and found solace in fantasy literature and
poetry. He would go on to study at Oxford and become a scholar of English
literature. Through the influence of Christian friends such as J. R. R. Tolkien
and Christian authors such as G. K. Chesterton, Lewis realized that
Scripture and the historic church had intelligent answers to modern questions. He returned to the Christian faith at age thirty-two.

During World War II, Lewis hosted a series of celebrated Christian radio
programs that offered hope and courage to the city of London during the Nazi
air raids. Lewis authored many books that continue to be read widely today,
including *Mere Christianity*, *The Screwtape Letters*, and The Chronicles of Narnia.
Together with old friends and companions such as Tolkien and Charles
Williams, Lewis formed the Inklings, an informal literary group that met rou-
tinely in an Oxford pub to share their writings and encourage future projects.
Lewis's *The Lion, the Witch, and the Wardrobe*, his Space Trilogy, Tolkien's The
Lord of the Rings, and many other fantasy and science fiction classics were
products of the camaraderie of this group. Memorable characters from Lewis's
books, like the Christlike lion Aslan and the demonic tempter Screwtape, have
captured the imaginations of Christians of all denominations.

Late in life, Lewis married American poet Joy Davidson. They were
married for four short years before Joy died of cancer in 1960. This loss
plunged Lewis into deep despair and a crisis of faith, which he recorded in
one of his final books, *A Grief Observed*. Lewis, the author of so many celebrated imaginative writings, realized that his own perceptions of God were
being refined and expanded in the midst of his grief. "My idea of God ... has
to be shattered time after time," Lewis wrote. "He shatters it Himself."[3] And
yet this shattering was not without hope. "Could we not almost say," Lewis
reflected, "that this shattering is one of the marks of His presence?" Lewis's
desire for Christ persisted until his final days. "I need Christ," Lewis concluded in *A Grief Observed*, "not something that resembles Him."[4]

SCRIPTURE

"Love does no wrong to a neighbor; therefore love is the fulfilling of the law." (Romans 13:10)

MEDITATION: OUR NEIGHBOR

What is your neighbor? At first blush, it appears I've used the wrong interrogative pronoun. Shouldn't we phrase the question, "Who is your neighbor?" Ah, but that's too easy to answer, isn't it? Your neighbor lives nearby. He is your coworker. She is next to you at the gym. He delivers your mail. She makes your coffee. Your neighbor is just as ordinary and common (and boring) as you.

Yes, yes, very good. But *what* is your neighbor?

According to the story of the Christian Bible, your neighbor is a remarkable creature. He or she is an eternal image-bearer of God that is uniquely imbued with dignity, honor, freedom, and worth. Your neighbor, in their very essence, possesses an aspect of divinity. As C. S. Lewis writes, "There are no ordinary people. You have never talked to a mere mortal."[5]

What would your interactions and relationships be like if you listened to, spoke to, and appreciated others *as they actually are*? Every brief interaction with another human being, no matter how seemingly inconsequential, would be pregnant with eternal, God-sourced meaning. Every relationship, from your mother-in-law to your college roommate, if it could be weighed, would tip the scales north of ten thousand metric tons.

Every neighbor, by virtue of their bearing the *imago Dei*, is worthy of love. Therefore, when God commands, in both the Old and New Testaments, that we are to love our neighbor, he commands that which would be natural if only we understood what our neighbor is.

PRAYER

Almighty God, we give you thanks for the ministry of C. S. Lewis, who labored that the church of Jesus Christ might be one. Grant that we, instructed by his teaching and example, and knit together in unity by your Spirit, may ever stand firm upon the one foundation, which is Jesus Christ our Lord, who lives and reigns with you, in the unity of the Holy Spirit, one God, now and forever. Amen.[6]

"BECAUSE OF THE INCARNATION, I SALUTE ALL REMAINING MATTER WITH REVERENCE."

MONK & TEACHER of the FAITH

JOHN of DAMASCUS c. 675–749

MONK AND TEACHER OF THE FAITH (c. 675–749)

Commemoration: December 4
Time: Seventh and eighth centuries
Place: Syria and Jerusalem

Because [of the incarnation,] I salute all remaining matter with reverence.[1]

THE COMING OF ISLAM IN THE SEVENTH CENTURY forever changed the Middle East, Northern Africa, and Europe, and John of Damascus was a Christian theologian who lived in this new reality. John was born in Damascus, Syria, to a prominent Arabic Christian family with the family name Mansur (which means "ransomed"). Syria had only recently been taken by Muslim conquest, and Arabic Christians grappled with how to live as conquered people under Islamic rule. The public profession of Christianity was forbidden by the new rulers, but John's father, Sarjun, enjoyed special liberties as a trusted treasurer for the Islamic caliph in Damascus.

One day, Sarjun witnessed a Christian slave about to be executed by Islamic slave traders. The slave was a former monk with an advanced education. Sarjun appealed to the caliph to allow the slave to live within his home. The caliph agreed, and the monk became John's tutor, giving the boy an advanced education. John studied Christian and Islamic literature deeply and, in adulthood, became a vocal defender of the Christian faith. In his monumental work *The Exposition of the Orthodox Faith*, John compiled the teachings of Scripture and the ancient church to create a systematic overview of critical Christian doctrines such as the Trinity, the incarnation, and the sacraments. This work sought to prepare Christians with answers to Muslim objections to the Christian faith.

John also prepared a defense of his beliefs for Christian critics, as well. In particular, he defended Christian iconography against the iconoclasts, a group of Christians who called for the destruction of artistic depictions of Jesus and the saints. Muslim critics also opposed Christian images. John asserted that the incarnation of Christ, as God made flesh, necessitated the depiction of Christ in artwork. Old Testament prohibitions of images of God came into new effect when God made an image of himself in Christ Jesus. John pointed to passages from Scripture like Colossians 1:15: "He is the image of the invisible God, the firstborn of all creation." John's theology was pivotal to the discussions of the Second Council of Nicaea (787), and John is regarded by many as a final figure in the age of the church fathers.

SCRIPTURE

"He is the image of the invisible God, the firstborn of all creation. For by him all things were created, in heaven and on earth, visible and invisible, whether thrones or dominions or rulers or authorities—all things were created through him and for him. And he is before all things, and in him all things hold together." (Colossians 1:15-17)

MEDITATION: SACRAMENTAL DIGNITY OF THE MATERIAL WORLD

Plato was right about many things, but the lingering effects of one of his errors persist today—dualism between the spiritual and the material. There remains a tendency for Christians today to separate the spiritual from the material and to prize spiritual things as more valuable than material things. This has led to all kinds of terrible abuses in Christian practice: evangelism prized over meeting the material needs of the poor, lengthy sermons prized over the bread and wine of Holy Communion, cognitive belief in orthodox doctrine prized over obedience to the commands of Jesus . . . and the long, frustrating list goes on. Left unchecked, this dualism develops into a kind of antimaterialistic Gnosticism. The shorthand might sound something like being "so heavenly minded that you're no earthly good."

But thankfully, God remains a materialist.

The material world was his idea and he's not about to give up on it anytime soon.

Consider that in his incarnation, the Son of God, the second person of the Holy Trinity, became a material creature. In Jesus, the spiritual and the material meet, overlap, and intersect. This not only gives tremendous credence to the value of all human life, but it also dignifies every atom in the material world. A right response might be seen in John of Damascus's words, "Because of the incarnation, I salute all remaining matter with reverence."

Of course, some of us are materialists in the worst sense of the word. We idolize material goods and pleasure and almost completely ignore the spiritual realm. But is the answer to slam materialism and become spiritualists? The incarnation of Jesus holds that over-reaction in check. Rather than requiring a choice between the spiritual and the material, the incarnation of Christ invites us to inhabit a sacramental world where the material is dignified without being idolized. This enables all followers of Jesus to receive and revere the material world for the gift it was always meant to be. What do you do when you receive a precious gift? You steward it with care.

Where do you have dualist tendencies? Are they toward the spiritual or the material? How might beholding the incarnation of Jesus reorient you toward both the spiritual and material realms of reality?

PRAYER

O Heavenly Father, who has filled the world with beauty, just as you opened the eyes of your servant John of Damascus, so open our eyes to behold your gracious hand in all your works, that, rejoicing in your whole creation, we may learn to serve you with gladness, for the sake of him by whom all things were made, your Son, Jesus Christ our Lord. Amen.[2]

BISHOP OF MYRA *(c. 270–343)*

Commemoration: December 6
Time: Third and fourth centuries
Place: Asia Minor (now Turkey)

The giver of every good and perfect gift has called upon us to mimic
His giving, by grace through faith, and this is not of ourselves.[1]

THE INSPIRATION FOR THE BELOVED SANTA CLAUS was a real, historical figure: Saint Nicholas. He was bishop of the seaport town of Myra (in modern-day Turkey) during Emperor Diocletian's widespread persecution of Christians in the late third and early fourth centuries. Nicholas was known for his generosity and compassion. After the death of his parents, Nicholas donated his inheritance to the poor. He cared for orphans and widows, giving gifts of food and providing the necessary money to prevent Christian children from being sold into slavery. So many acts of mercy and miraculous deliverance are attributed to Nicholas that he is sometimes known by his nickname, Nicholas the Wonderworker.

Diocletian's successor, Constantine, declared an end to the persecution and granted toleration for Christianity, but threats to the church soon came from within. The priest Arius began teaching that Jesus Christ was not coeternal with the Father but was instead a divine hero and a created being. Nicholas believed that Arius's teaching was a corruption of the faith handed down by the apostles and suffered for by the early church martyrs.

The Council of Nicaea was called in 325 to address Arius's teaching. Nicholas was among the three hundred bishops and nearly two thousand clergy in attendance. Emotions ran high at the council, as many in attendance bore the scars and wounds of Diocletian's persecution. Legendary accounts of the council say that Nicholas, having witnessed so many children and innocents suffering for their true faith in Christ, was overcome with emotion when he saw Arius present at the council. Walking up to Arius, he slapped the false teacher across the face. Nicholas was arrested for the assault, and the elderly bishop spent the remainder of the council in a prison cell.

Nicholas's fierce dedication to theological accuracy was matched by his fierce devotion and love for children. The memory of Nicholas has been cherished through the centuries, and he is known today in many regions of the world as Santa Claus (derived from *Sint Nikolaas*, a Dutch name for Saint Nicholas).

SCRIPTURE

"Every good and perfect gift is from above, coming down from the Father of lights, with whom there is no variation or shadow due to change. Of his own will he brought us forth by the word of truth, that we should be a kind of firstfruits of his creatures." (James 1:17-18)

MEDITATION: THE ART OF GIVING

When Ebenezer Scrooge faces his own mortality, the dead-end terminus of his miserly greed, he converts. He renounces his old self and puts on a new self. What if he had only converted in his heart? What if he had decided to merely *believe* in selfless generosity without practicing it? Well, of course it would be evidence that no substantive change had occurred. It also would make a really lousy story. The delightful conclusion of Dickens's *A Christmas Carol* is the exuberant, unrestricted, overflowing generosity that bursts forth from Scrooge's changed heart. What does it mean that one of Western society's most beloved mythologies is about money?

Might it suggest that somehow, we all know deep in our bones that true heart change is always demonstrated by generous giving?

It is no exaggeration to say that money is God's arch competitor for human allegiance. For perhaps the majority in the American church today, materialism remains the primary barrier to progressing from spiritual infancy to maturity. Tragically, many Christians have known the Lord for years, even decades ... but they have never modeled biblical generosity themselves. So they remain babies in Christ, with the most important step in sanctification still lying ahead of them.[2]

Saint Nicholas was not generous because he wanted kids to like him or because it was merely fun to give presents. He was giving what he had already received, and continued to receive, from his heavenly Father. His generosity was but a shadow of the true generosity that God had showed him in the gospel.

There may be such a thing as a generous unbeliever who practices the virtue from a heart of gratitude, even if they do not know that their gratitude is owed to Jesus. But there is no such creature as an ungenerous or stingy Christian. It is a contradiction in terms. A Christian who does not give their money away freely and generously has yet to truly convert.

PRAYER

O merciful Creator, you inspired the generosity of your servant Nicholas, and your loving hand is open wide to satisfy the needs of every living creature: Make us always thankful for your loving providence, and give us grace to honor you with all that you have entrusted to us; that we, remembering the account we must one day give, may be faithful stewards of your good gifts; through Jesus Christ our Lord, who with you and the Holy Spirit lives and reigns, one God, for ever and ever. Amen.[3]

MARTYR *(c. 283–304)*

Commemoration: December 13
Time: Third and fourth centuries
Place: Sicily (Italy)

I bless you, O Father of my Lord Jesus Christ, because through your Son the fire has no power over me.[1]

THE LIGHT OF CHRIST SHONE SO BRILLIANTLY in the life of Lucy that not even the darkness of blindness and death could overcome it. Lucy ("Santa Lucia") was a young Christian in Syracuse, Sicily, who lived and died during the great persecution of Emperor Diocletian. Most of the other details of her life have been lost to history, but legendary accounts of her life have been passed down through the generations. It is said that at great risk to her own safety, Lucy brought provisions to the poor, the sick, and Christians in hiding. She made these trips of mercy in the dead of night with a crown of candles around her head that lit her way as she traveled with arms full of food.

During this time, her widowed mother suffered from a blood hemorrhage; fearing her imminent death, she arranged for Lucy to marry a pagan suitor. Lucy pointed her mother to the gospel story in which Jesus cured a woman with a similar affliction. Together, they prayed, and Lucy's mother was healed. In thanksgiving, Lucy gave a substantial portion of her dowry to the poor. When Lucy's fiancé discovered that the dowry had been donated away, he was enraged. He reported Lucy as a Christian to Roman authorities. The authorities demanded that Lucy renounce Christ, and when she refused, she was condemned to a life of prostitution. But when the soldiers laid hands on Lucy to drag her away, a miraculous power made Lucy immovable. Her eyes were then put out and she was set aflame. When the fire failed to harm her, Lucy gave praise to God, and she was killed with a sword.

Lucy's victory in Christ and her courageous faith have been remembered by every generation of Christians since her martyrdom. Her commemoration day falls in the dark days before the winter solstice, when the daylight of the Northern Hemisphere continues to grow shorter with each passing day. Yet her name, Lucy (or Lucia), means light, and her feast day is associated with Advent, which anticipates the coming of the true light of Christ into the world, which forever dispels the darkness. Traditional depictions of Lucy show her crowned in candles and staring with resurrected eyes while she triumphantly holds her eyes on a platter of gold.

SCRIPTURE

"The light shines in the darkness, and the darkness has not overcome it." (John 1:5)

MEDITATION: DRIVE OUT THE DARKNESS

Darkness is not a presence, but an absence. Darkness has no substance. It is a terrible void, an abyss of nothing. Evil metastasizes in the darkness, and when light breaks through, evil screams its shameful, vengeful protest. Evil requires darkness to shut out, smother, obliterate the light; otherwise it will writhe in the agony of exposure and shrivel away into oblivion.

A truly virtuous person is like a candle lit in a dark room. The match is struck, the sulfur flares, and shadows jump away to the walls. If the flame burns brighter, and if more candles are lit, soon light will penetrate every nook and cranny with a brightness from which no shadow can hide. This is why the pure in heart, the humble and meek, the generous and good are so often persecuted when they are young. The evil in this world will not risk the virtuous youth growing into a fully mature adult. There may be no stopping them then. So kill 'em while they're young, before they can do much damage; before their light burns too bright.

Lucy's goodness burned incandescent and was therefore a threat to the lust, greed, and control of the empire. Sentencing a young Christian girl to prostitution was an attempt to corrupt and pollute that which was pure. The miracle of her immovability was a kind of physical manifestation of the immovability of her spirit. It was the glimpse of a moment when darkness could not overcome the light.

Lucy's light in the darkness was but a signpost to the true light that has come and is coming into the world. In Advent, the faithful church remembers the first coming of the Messiah and leans forward in anticipation of his second coming.

At the birth of Christ, a match was struck. And though the agony of the cross sought to extinguish the light, the resurrection on Easter rekindled the flame. Now more and more candles are being lit as the faith is passed from soul to soul, from generation to generation.

It may seem, at times, that the darkness is winning; but that is a fiction. Even if a few candles are snuffed out here and there, dawn is on its way. Sunbeams of divine laughter will break over the horizon, and darkness will curse and flee in vain.

Until then, we keep watch.

Darkness o'er the city lies

Dark our hearts, dark our eyes

Dark our own divine estate

Dark our dreams of late

Come Lord Jesus,

Be our light!

PRAYER

Almighty God, just as you gave your grace to your daughter Lucy, so give us grace to cast away the works of darkness and put on the armor of light, now in the time of this mortal life in which your Son Jesus Christ came to visit us in great humility; that in the last day, when he shall come again in his glorious majesty to judge both the living and the dead, we may rise to the life immortal, through him who lives and reigns with you and the Holy Spirit, one God, now and forever. Amen.[2]

MISSIONARY *(c. 296–c. 338)*

Commemoration: December 15
Time: Fourth century
Place: Cappadocia (now Turkey), Jerusalem, and Georgia

O Lord, send down your mercy upon this nation, that all nations may glorify you alone, the one true God, through your son, Jesus Christ.[1]

NINO (ALSO KNOWN AS NINA), the Enlightener of Georgia, was a courageous missionary in the ancient church who bore the light of Christ to a distant land, driven by the love of Christ for the lost. She was born in Cappadocia (now Turkey) and raised in Jerusalem during the great persecution of Emperor Diocletian. As a child, she learned of the faraway land of Georgia, on the far east of the Black Sea in the Caucasus Mountains. Nino's heart was mysteriously drawn to that pagan land, with a desire to see the gospel reach the Georgian people. In a climate of harsh persecution and grave danger, Nino made the great journey to Georgia. Having learned Hebrew in Jerusalem, Nino sheltered with a Jewish community in Georgia. There, the Jewish residents taught Nino about the culture and practices of the pagan Georgians. Nino was grieved to see so many of the Georgians living in fear and cowering before their pagan idols. She prayed, "O Lord, send down Thy mercy upon this nation . . . that all nations may glorify Thee alone, the One True God, through Thy Son, Jesus Christ."[2] In answer to this prayer, a hailstorm arose and the idols were destroyed.

Nino courageously preached the gospel to large crowds, holding a cross bound by the strands of her hair. Many converted because of Nino's teaching, and her name soon became known to all, including Mirian, king of the Georgians. Mirian was a devoted pagan and was perplexed by the sudden surge of conversions to Christianity. One day, while he was out hunting, he resolved to order an extermination of all Christians in his kingdom. But once he was resolved to carry out this wicked plan, a darkness fell across his mind and he was consumed with terror. He prayed in desperation to all of his gods and could find no relief. As a final resort, he prayed to Christ. "God of Nino," Mirian prayed, "illumine this night for me and guide my footsteps, and I will declare Thy Holy Name. I will erect a cross and venerate it and I will construct for Thee a temple. I vow to be obedient to Nino and to the Faith of the Roman people!"[3] Mirian was delivered from his darkness, and he declared that his kingdom would henceforth be dedicated to the faith of Nino.

SCRIPTURE

"Be subject for the Lord's sake to every human institution, whether it be to the emperor as supreme, or to governors as sent by him to punish those who do evil and to praise those who do good. For this is the will of God, that by doing good you should put to silence the ignorance of foolish people. Live as people who are free, not using your freedom as a cover-up for evil, but living as servants of God. Honor everyone. Love the brotherhood. Fear God. Honor the emperor." (1 Peter 2:13-17)

MEDITATION: THE HEART OF CHIRSTIAN PATRIOTISM

In seeking to love and serve a country to which she was not native, Nino shows us the heart of Christian patriotism (which is fascinating, because the country Nino served was not one to which she was native). The Christian patriot seeks the good of a country and recognizes that, to do so, they must resist and even undermine the established idols that are harming the country. This will earn the Christian patriot the exact opposite label that they seek—they will be accused of being a bad citizen.

In order to be truly faithful as a Christian patriot, the follower of Jesus must be willing to endure the opposition, accusations, and persecution that will inevitably come against them if they seek the good of their country. You cannot seek someone's good and seek to be *liked* by them at the same time. You can have one or the other, not both. Case in point: to be a good parent and seek the well-being of your child, you must be willing to endure your kid not liking you.

The path of being a good patriot and citizen and the path of following Jesus are one and the same, though you should not expect the state to recognize and affirm this. Christians are to be good citizens that seek the well-being of their country, but they will not be seen as such if the powers that be are running an unjust empire.

What kinds of idols are wreaking havoc in your country? What gods and goddesses overpromize and underdeliver to your fellow citizens? How might you practice the subversive love of Jesus and undermine the idols of your land to offer something better in their place?

It is a good thing to love your country. To love your country well, you must not idolize it or share in its idol worship. Therefore, loving your country will often require a prophetic witness against your country.

Remember, God sends his prophets to the ones he loves. Jonah didn't want to bear prophetic witness to Nineveh because he didn't want God to love Nineveh. God sent prophets to his own people, not because he hated his own country, but because he loved Israel and desired their good. Prophetic confrontation is often required for faithful patriotism.

PRAYER

Almighty God, who by your Son called the evangelists, giving them grace to preach the gospel to the ends of the earth, grant to us also your grace, that we may hold fast their doctrine and, following their example and the example of your servant Nino, set forward your kingdom, through Jesus Christ, your Son our Lord, who lives and reigns with you in the unity of the Holy Spirit, one God, world without end. Amen.[4]

APPENDIX A

CHURCH HISTORY SURVEY

THIS BRIEF SUMMARY OF CHURCH HISTORY is provided so that you can easily place where the saints in this book fit into the overall two-thousand-year story of church history.

THE RESURRECTION (AD 33)

Jesus was born into a world that was yearning for hope. Jews hoped for liberation from the oppressive empires of the Gentiles (non-Jewish people). Gentiles hoped to maintain military, social, and economic dominance. Into this tension, Jesus proclaimed a hope that challenged the paradigms of both the Jews and the Gentiles. Jesus spoke of forgiveness of sins, restored unity with God, and a coming kingdom. Conspiring together, the Gentiles and the Jews killed Jesus in the cruelest form of execution known to the ancient world: crucifixion. Jesus suffered and died. And then the unthinkable happened: God raised Jesus from the grave, from the dead, defeating sin and death and ushering true hope into the world. He commissioned his disciples to go into all the world, announcing the good news (the gospel) of his resurrection and coming kingdom and baptizing in the name of the Father and the Son and the Holy Spirit. After forty days with his disciples, the resurrected Jesus ascended into heaven, with the promise that he would return.

APOSTLES (FIRST CENTURY)

Ten days after Jesus' ascension, the Holy Spirit descended on the disciples at Pentecost and empowered them to obey Jesus' command to go into all the world, baptizing in the name of the Father, the Son, and the Holy Spirit. Pentecost is considered the birth of the New Testament church. The first disciples journeyed to every corner of the known world. From Ethiopia to India, from Egypt to Armenia, from Syria to Spain, these first-century disciples obeyed Jesus' Great Commission. They proclaimed the good news of Jesus' resurrection, baptized new believers, and planted churches centered around the Word and the Table ("the Lord's Supper").

EARLY MARTYRS AND EARLY MISSIONARIES (FIRST CENTURY–FOURTH CENTURY)

Wherever churches were planted, rumors developed about the identity of this new community called Christians. One rumor claimed that Christians were cannibals because it was said that they were eating and drinking someone's body and blood in a central act of worship called the Eucharist. Another rumor said that Christians were insurrectionists because they called a man named Jesus their Lord and God instead of Caesar or any other earthly ruler. Starting in the first century, state-authorized persecution broke out against the church. It began to be said that "the blood of the martyrs [was] the seed of the church,"[1] because as more and more Christians gave their lives for Christ, more and more people became Christians. Converts were especially numerous among classes of people for whom ancient society offered little hope. Women, slaves, and servants came to Christ in especially large numbers in these early centuries. Soon, even the homes of the wealthy and politically powerful were filled with Christian servants and slaves. In the Roman Empire, this resulted in a bottom-up conversion of society that came to fruition in 313 when Emperor Constantine announced that he had become a Christian, and the state-authorized persecution of Christians was abolished.

Early martyrs and early missionaries in this book include Polycarp (ch. 10), Justin (ch. 26), Margaret of Antioch (ch. 32), Lucy (ch. 51), Perpetua and Felicity (ch. 11), Nino of Georgia (ch. 52), Valentine (ch. 7), and Patrick (ch. 13).

THE CHURCH COUNCILS (FOURTH–EIGHTH CENTURY)

When Constantine converted to Christianity, he had questions. In his time, a false teaching about Jesus became popular in certain churches around the Mediterranean. This teaching, called Arianism, taught that Jesus was not the divine and eternal creator, but was instead a divine hero and the first creation of God the Father. This teaching contradicted the apostolic faith that had been preserved by the church. To settle this issue, in 325 Constantine invited church representatives from across the known world to meet in the resort town of Nicaea (in modern-day Turkey) to discuss: is Jesus a divine hero, or the divine and eternal Creator? Influential figures were present at the council, like the deacon and theologian Athanasius of Egypt and the bishop and benefactor of poor children, Nicholas of Myra (the historical figure behind Santa Claus). After the discussion, a vote was held, and the result wasn't even close: the council affirmed that Jesus was coeternal and of one substance with God the Father and with the Holy Spirit. Jesus was the second person of the Trinity, the same Trinity in whose name Jesus had commanded his disciples to baptize. The conclusions of the Council of Nicaea (325)—as affirmed and expanded by the subsequent Council of Constantinople (381)—were summarized in the Nicene Creed. Christians have recited the Nicene Creed as a statement of faith ever since. In later centuries, the church held additional significant councils that continued to discuss and define the apostolic faith. These councils are called the ecumenical councils. The teachers who contributed to the theology of these early centuries are called the church fathers and mothers.

Church fathers and mothers from the age of the ecumenical councils in this book include Nicholas of Myra (ch. 50), Athanasius (ch. 21), Gregory of Nazianzus (ch. 1), Macrina (ch. 31), Augustine and Monica (ch. 35), Mary of Egypt (ch. 15), and John of Damascus (ch. 49).

MONASTICS (THIRD CENTURY-PRESENT)

During the age of the church fathers and mothers, some Christians began meeting in communities called monasteries, centering their lives on organized schedules of prayer and work (in Latin, *ora et labora*). Inspired by the practices of ancient Jewish prayer communities, Christians in monasteries stopped and prayed at eight specific hours of the day and then devoted themselves to various forms of work as an outflowing and application of their prayers.

The earliest monastic communities were organized in Africa, in the deserts and wilderness of Egypt. The monastic model soon spread to the Middle East, Eastern Europe, Asia, and even the distant British Isles. Benedict of Nursia and his sister Scholastica organized a monastic model particularly influential in Western Europe. Monastic communities devoted themselves to work in the arts, the sciences, and theology. Musical notation, natural sciences, modern genetics, and many other academic fields originated in monastic work. Many institutions we now consider integral to an advanced society have their roots in monasticism, including hospitals, universities, schools, and orphanages. Monastics also devoted their time to hand-copying Scripture, poetry, and ancient manuscripts of science and philosophy. While the ancient world was falling away in the Roman Empire, monasteries were not only preserving learning and civilization but cultivating it.

Monastic saints in this book include Moses the Ethiopian (ch. 28), Benedict and Scholastica (ch. 29), Herman of Alaska (ch. 46), and Josephine Bakhita (ch. 5).

SCHISM (FIFTH-ELEVENTH CENTURY)

The collapse of Roman civilization was evident in the year 452 when Attila the Hun gathered with his barbarian army around the city of Rome and threatened to loot and destroy it. The Roman government had deteriorated, and the city lay defenseless. In their hour of need, the Romans turned to the last credible institution in Rome—the church. The bishop of Rome, Leo I, affectionately called the papa or the pope, heard the cry of his city. He courageously met Attila the Hun face-to-face and convinced the barbarian warlord to spare the city. At a time of crisis, the pope filled a political vacuum.

Over the next several centuries, occupants of the papal chair made increasing claims about the supremacy of the pope over both church and state worldwide. Many churches in Western Europe accepted this religious and political power structure. For example, in the seventh century, the church in England agreed to abandon their ancient Celtic worship traditions for Roman worship.

Churches outside Western Europe pushed back against many of the pope's claims for authority. The pope attempted to alter the Nicene Creed by adding a new word (*filioque* in Latin, translating to "and of the Son"). Eastern Christians refused to accept this decision. Western Christians disfellowshiped Eastern Christians in 1054, and the Eastern Christians did the same to the West. The global church was officially torn in two in the Great Schism. The church in Western Europe became known as the Roman

Catholic Church. The churches of the East became known as the Eastern Orthodox Church. The Great Schism was a great tragedy for the church. Before, the churches of the West and of the East had held each other accountable. Now they went their separate ways.

Saints in this book who served the church during the growing schism include Alcuin (ch. 24), Olga and Vladimir (ch. 30), Hilda of Whitby (ch. 47), and Cyril and Methodius (ch. 7).

MEDIEVAL CRISIS AND RENEWAL (ELEVENTH–SIXTEENTH CENTURY)

The centuries following the Great Schism were a period when Western Europeans made some disturbing deviations from the true message of the gospel, deviations that modern popes have formally acknowledged and of which they have formally repented. The atrocities of the Crusades and the horrors of the Inquisition, the theological justification for slavery and colonialism . . . all of these manifested in the Western church in the centuries following the Great Schism. The medieval Roman Catholic Church fell into corruption, and some medieval popes and clergy grappled for dominance and wealth in the Western church's political power structure. In some areas of Western Europe, the language of the people was banned from worship and only Latin was allowed. During this period, voices of concern pushed back against different dimensions of church life. Francis of Assisi and Clare of Assisi called the church to remember Christ's humility and renounce the pursuit of worldly power and wealth. John Wycliffe, an English priest, taught that every English person should hear God's Word and the church's liturgy in their own language. Voices of dissent, concern, and reform escalated.

Saints of the medieval church include Hildegard of Bingen (ch. 39), Francis of Assisi (ch. 41), Thomas Aquinas (ch. 3), Julian of Norwich (ch. 22), Catherine of Siena (ch. 19), and Joan of Arc (ch. 25).

REFORMATION (SIXTEENTH–SEVENTEENTH CENTURY)

In 1517, an Augustinian monk named Martin Luther nailed his Ninety-Five Theses of protest to the door of his local church. Representatives of the Roman Catholic Church were charging people money for time out of purgatory to raise funds for a church building construction project. This practice was a step too far for Martin Luther, and he challenged church officials to answer for this abuse. Instead of debating Luther, the pope excommunicated him. The Protestant Reformation had begun.

Luther taught that salvation was by grace alone, through faith alone, in Christ alone. The pope and the Roman Catholic Church would soon issue their own reforms to address medieval abuses in the church, but not before Martin Luther's teachings caught on like wildfire throughout Europe. Before long, individuals and entire kingdoms began breaking out of the pope's political power structure.

England, ruled by King Henry VIII, was the largest kingdom to break from Rome. The Church of England was shepherded by Archbishop of Canterbury Thomas Cranmer, an admirer of Martin Luther and a friend of European reformers like John Calvin. Like John Wycliffe centuries before him, Cranmer envisioned the liturgy and Scripture translated into English and available to every man, woman, and child in England. Cranmer compiled the prayers and liturgies from Scripture and church history and bound them into the Book of Common Prayer. The Book of Common Prayer and the English Bible were distributed throughout England. This resulted in a flowering of English literacy and culture. In the coming centuries, this culture would go global with the dawn of the British Empire.

Christians who spread the gospel during the Reformation era include William Tyndale (ch. 42), Paul Miki (ch. 4), Kateri Tekakwitha (ch. 18), John Bunyan (ch. 36), Teresa of Ávila (ch. 44), and Martin of Porres (ch. 45).

REVIVALS (EIGHTEENTH-TWENTIETH CENTURY)

As Western European culture went global, so did the influence of European society. Roman Catholics, Church of England Anglicans, and Protestant denominations like Presbyterians and Baptists all planted churches across the globe. However, evils of European society, like the transatlantic slave trade, also expanded. Eighteenth-century pastors like the Anglican brothers and founders of the Methodist movement, John and Charles Wesley, urged Christians to seek salvation, pursue personal holiness, and allow that holiness to reform society. Inspired by this message, an age of evangelical social renewal dawned. Member of Parliament William Wilberforce and freed African slave Olaudah Equiano devoted their lives to speaking against slavery. Their efforts brought about the abolition of the British slave trade. Other evangelical movements pursued global evangelization, reform for prisons and the judicial system, and alleviating poverty and alcoholism. This period of reform and spiritual renewal is known as the Great Awakening, and its influence continues to shape our world today. Inspired by these early social renewal efforts, the Christian church later continued to struggle for dignity and justice for minorities, women, and the oppressed in the nineteenth and twentieth centuries.

Saints in this book from the age of the Great Awakening revivals include Absalom Jones (ch. 6), Harriet Tubman (ch. 12), Olaudah Equiano and William Wilberforce (ch. 34), and Johann Sebastian Bach (ch. 33).

MODERNISM (EIGHTEENTH-TWENTIETH CENTURY)

Starting in the late eighteenth century, many people noted dramatic societal advancements and discerned that humanity was entering a new age. Instead of attributing these advancements to the fruits of the gospel, many people in Europe and America credited this progress to mere human ingenuity. Many intellectuals assumed divisions between faith and reason, God and science, and the individual and the community. In the West, historic universities and cultural institutions founded by Christians began to embrace modernist, secularist ideas. Throughout the nineteenth and twentieth centuries, this trend continued and accelerated. Secular totalitarian regimes sought to exterminate religion altogether and put millions to death, including Lutheran pastor Dietrich Bonhoeffer and Roman Catholic priest Maximilian Kolbe. Academic secularists combated religion with a softer approach but communicated that Christian orthodoxy was irrelevant to modern life. Christian intellectuals like G. K. Chesterton and C. S. Lewis called people to remember that Scripture and the historic church had answers to modern questions. Unfortunately, by the end of the twentieth century, many historic Christian denominations in Western Europe and North America had drifted far from Christian orthodoxy and embraced secular modernism, and the overall population of Christianity in the West began to shrink rapidly.

Important saints of the modern era in this book include Óscar Romero (ch. 14), Martin Luther King Jr. (ch. 16), Dietrich Bonhoeffer (ch. 17), C. S. Lewis (ch. 48), and Teresa of Calcutta (ch. 38).

GLOBAL REALIGNMENT (TWENTY-FIRST CENTURY)

If you only focus on the state of the church in the West at the end of the twentieth century, it's easy to get discouraged. But the church's story has never been merely the story of Western civilization. Just as the ancient church before the Great Schism of 1054 held itself accountable between the East and the West, today, Christians in the Global North (Western Europe and North America) are held accountable by Christians in the Global South (Africa, Latin America, and Asia). A century ago, most Christians lived in the North, with two-thirds of global Christians in Europe.[2] Since that time, the overall number of Christians has quadrupled amid a century of population growth and dedicated foreign and indigenous missionary work.

Today the largest population of Christians live in the Global South,[3] with more than twice the number of Christians worldwide in the Global South compared to the Global North. One in every four Christians now live in sub-Saharan Africa.[4] More Anglicans attend Sunday services in Nigeria than in all of North America and Great Britain combined.[5] Brazil has a larger population of Roman Catholics than any country on earth.[6] By 2030, China is projected to be the nation with the world's largest Christian population.[7] By 2050, the number of Christians in the Global South is projected to outnumber those in the North by three to one.[8]

Global South Christians are largely defined by an adherence to Christian orthodoxy, a reliance on the Holy Spirit, and a resistance to Western secularism. This global realignment has altered the gravitational pull of Christian culture. Global South churches now send missionaries to North America and Europe to remind Global North Christians of the truth and relevance of the historic, apostolic faith. African, South American, and Asian brothers and sisters are powerful voices and witnesses of God's faithfulness as we all serve the Lord and await his return.

Saints in this book who contributed to the global realignment include Mary Slessor (ch. 2), Agnes Tsao Kou Ying, Lucy Yi Zhenmei, Agatha Lin Zhao (ch. 9), the Martyrs of Sudan (ch. 23), Andrew Kim Taegon (ch. 40), Sundar Singh (ch. 27), Pandita Mary Ramabai (ch. 20), Lucian Tapiedi (ch. 37), Esther John (ch. 43), and Janani Luwum (ch. 8).

CHRONOLOGICAL LISTING OF SAINTS

FIFTEENTH AND SIXTEENTH CENTURIES

EIGHTEENTH AND NINETEENTH CENTURIES

TWENTIETH AND TWENTY-FIRST CENTURIES

APPENDIX C
GEOGRAPHIC LISTING OF SAINTS

AFRICA

AMERICAS

EAST ASIA AND OCEANIA

MIDDLE EAST/EASTERN EUROPE

43   Polycarp (c. 69–c. 155), Bishop of Smyrna and Martyr

105   Justin (c. 100–c. 165), Teacher of the Faith and Martyr

196   Nicholas ("Santa Claus") (c. 270–343), Bishop of Myra

129   Margaret of Antioch (c. 289–c. 305), Martyr

204   Nino of Georgia (c. 296–c. 338), Missionary

125   Macrina (c. 327–379), Nun and Teacher of the Faith

9   Gregory of Nazianzus (c. 329–390), Bishop of Constantinople and Teacher of the Faith

192   John of Damascus (c. 675–749), Monk and Teacher of the Faith

33   Methodius (815–885), Missionary

33   Cyril (826–869), Missionary

121   Olga (c. 890–969), Patron of the Church in Russia and Ukraine

121   Vladimir (c. 953–1015), Patron of the Church in Russia and Ukraine

WESTERN EUROPE

33   Valentine (c. 226–c. 269), Valentine Martyr

200   Lucy (c. 283–304), Martyr

54   Patrick (c. 385–c. 461), Bishop and Missionary

117   Benedict (c. 480–c. 547), Monastic Leader

117   Scholastica (c. 480–c. 543), Monastic Leader

185   Hilda of Whitby (c. 614–680), Abbess

98   Alcuin (c. 735–804), Deacon and Abbot of Tours

155   Hildegard (c. 1098–1179), Abbess of Bingen

163   Francis of Assisi (c. 1182–1226), Friar, Deacon, and Reformer of the Church

17   Thomas Aquinas (1225–1274), Friar, Priest, and Teacher of the Faith

90   Julian of Norwich (c. 1343–c. 1416), Theologian

78   Catherine of Siena (1347–1380), Reformer of the Church

102   Joan of Arc (c. 1412–1431), Visionary

167   William Tyndale (c. 1494–1536), Priest, Translator of the Bible, and Martyr

174   Teresa of Ávila (1515–1582), Teacher of the Faith

143   John Bunyan (1628–1688), Teacher of the Faith

132   Johann Sebastian Bach (1685–1750), Composer

136   William Wilberforce (1759–1833), Renewer of Society

189   Clive Staples Lewis (1898–1963), Teacher of the Faith

70   Dietrich Bonhoeffer (1906–1945), Pastor and Martyr

ACKNOWLEDGMENTS

THIS BOOK IS INDEBTED to a great cloud of witnesses who offered hours of careful insight, gracious criticism, and encouragement. We are especially grateful to our wives, Bethany Lansing and Rachel Marotta, who lovingly supported our work on this book from the start.

I (Marotta) also want to thank my dear children: June, Selah Rose, Wills, and John for their gracious patience with me as writing this book took away from family time together. I love and am proud of each you.

We want to thank the dear people of Redeemer Anglican Church. It is a gift to minister among such excellent brothers and sisters.

We are also very grateful to the many online readers from around the globe, whose support and encouragement has helped to shape the Our Church Speaks project since its inception.

Special thanks also go to the many scholars who contributed their time and talents as they reviewed this book's manuscript, including Gregory Strong, PhD (Former Adjunct Faculty in Anglican Studies at Reformed Theological Seminary, northern Virginia campus); Caleb Maskell, PhD (professor of religion at Princeton University and Executive Secretary of the American Society of Church History); Alex Fogleman, PhD (research professor of theology at Baylor University); and the Reverend Justin Hendrix (priest at Church of the Incarnation in Henrico, Virginia).

We are grateful to our agent, Don Gates, and to our editor, Al Hsu, for affirming our vision for this book and for their patient insights and suggestions.

This book and the Our Church Speaks project as a whole are better because of these dedicated friends and family members.

NOTES

INTRODUCTION: SAINTS OVER CELEBRITIES

[1] C. S. Lewis, *God in the Dock* (Grand Rapids, MI: Eerdmans, 1970), 203–4.
[2] The basic structure and wording for this liturgy is inspired by the Daily Office and Family Prayer from *Book of Common Prayer* (Huntington Beach, CA: Anglican Liturgy Press, 2019), 21, 26, 67–74.

1. GREGORY OF NAZIANZUS

[1] Philip Schaff and Henry Wace, eds., *A Select Library of Nicene and Post-Nicene Fathers of the Christian Church*, vol. 7 (Peabody, MA: Hendrickson Publishers, 2012), 187–200, 1,886–89.
[2] Gregory of Nazianzus, *On God and Christ: The Five Theological Orations and Two Letters to Cledonius*, Popular Patristics vol. 23, trans. Frederick Williams and Lionel Wickham (Yonkers, NY: St. Vladimir's Seminary Press, 2002).
[3] Brian Matz, *Gregory of Nazianzus*, Foundations of Theological Exegesis and Christian Spirituality (Grand Rapids, MI: Baker Academic, 2016).
[4] Robert Atwell and Christopher L. Webber, eds., *Celebrating the Saints: Devotional Readings for Saint's Days* (Harrisburg, PA: Morehouse Publishing, 2001), 154–55.
[5] Adapted from the commemoration "Of a Teacher of the Faith," *Book of Common Prayer* (Huntington Beach, CA: Anglican Liturgy Press, 2019), 638.

2. MARY SLESSOR

[1] Frederick Quinn, *African Saints: Saints, Martyrs, and Holy People from the Continent of Africa* (New York: The Crossroads Publishing Company, 2002), 179.
[2] Fung Yu-Lan, *A History of Chinese Philosophy* (Princeton, NJ: Princeton University Press, 1952), 327.
[3] Adapted from "Prayer for All Missionaries," *Book of Common Prayer* (Huntington Beach, CA: Anglican Liturgy Press, 2019), 652.

3. THOMAS AQUINAS

[1] "Feast of Saint Thomas Aquinas," Aquinas Institute of Rochester, January 28, 2016, www.aquinasinstitute.com/news-detail?pk=1065424.
[2] Robert E. Barron, *Thomas Aquinas: Spiritual Master* (New York: The Crossroad Publishing Company, 1996), 20.
[3] Josef Pieper, *Guide to Thomas Aquinas* (San Francisco: Ignatius Press, 1962), 20.
[4] As translated in "St. Thomas's Last Days," The Sacra Doctrina Project, https://thomistica.net/st-thomas-last-days.
[5] "For a Virtuous Heart," *Book of Common Prayer* (Huntington Beach, CA: Anglican Liturgy Press, 2019), 674.

4. PAUL MIKI

[1] *The Liturgy of the Hours, Lenten Season, Easter Season* (New York: Catholic Book Publishing, 1976), 1,664.
[2] John Dougill, *In Search of Japan's Hidden Christians: A Story of Suppression, Secrecy and Survival* (London: Society for Promoting Christian Knowledge, 2016).
[3] "St. Paul Miki and Companions," Catholic News Agency, www.catholicnewsagency.com/saint/st-paul-miki-and-companions-139.
[4] George Zabelka, "Blessing the Bombs," *Plough*, August 9, 2022, www.plough.com/en/topics/justice/nonviolence/blessing-the-bombs.

[5]"Prayer for Desiring God," *Book of Common Prayer* (Huntington Beach, CA: Anglican Liturgy Press, 2019), 668.

5. JOSEPHINE BAKHITA

[1]Pope Benedict XVI, Encyclical Letter *Spe Salvi* ("Saved in Hope"), November 30, 2007, www.vatican.va/content/benedict-xvi/en/encyclicals/documents/hf_ben-xvi_enc _20071130_spe-salvi.html.

[2]Roberto Italo Zanini, *Bakhita: From Slave to Saint* (San Francisco: Ignatius Press, 2010), 81.

[3]J. Hart, "Come, Ye Sinners," 1759.

[4]Adapted from the prayer "For the Discouraged and Downcast," *Book of Common Prayer* (Huntington Beach, CA: Anglican Liturgy Press, 2019), 663.

6. ABSALOM JONES

[1]Absalom Jones, "A Thanksgiving Sermon" in *American Sermons: The Pilgrims to Martin Luther King, Jr.*, Michael Warner, ed. (New York: Penguin Putnam, 1999), 543.

[2]"The Great Walkout," St. Thomas African Episcopal Church, www.aecst.org/walkout.htm.

[3]Mark Sidwell, "The First Heroes of African American Christianity," *Christianity Today*, issue 62, 1999, www.christianitytoday.com/history/issues/issue-62/black-christianity-before -civil-war-gallery--fruit-of.html.

[4]Adapted from the prayer "To Please God Rather than Men," *Book of Common Prayer* (Huntington Beach, CA: Anglican Liturgy Press, 2019), 669.

7. VALENTINE, CYRIL, AND METHODIUS

[1]"St. Valentine," Encyclopedia Britannica, last modified February 14, 2024, www.britannica .com/biography/Saint-Valentine.

[2]John Paul II, Encyclical Letter *Slavorum Apostoli*, June 2, 1985, www.vatican.va/content /john-paul-ii/en/encyclicals/documents/hf_jp-ii_enc_19850602_slavorum-apostoli .html#%24G.

[3]"The Hymn of Cyril & Methodius" in *Anglican Breviary* (New York: The Frank Gavin Liturgical Foundation, 1998), E290.

[4]Michael Walsh, ed., *Butler's Lives of the Saints, Concise Edition* (San Francisco: Harper & Row, 1985).

[5]Sally Lloyd-Jones, *The Jesus Storybook Bible* (Grand Rapids, MI: Zondervan, 2007).

[6]Adapted from *Book of Common Prayer* (Huntington Beach, CA: Anglican Liturgy Press, 2019), 640.

8. JANANI LUWUM

[1]Henry Luke Orombi, "What Is Anglicanism," *First Things*, August 2007, www.firstthings.com /article/2007/08/001-what-is-anglicanism.

[2]"Faith and Conflict: The Global Rise of Christianity," Council on Foreign Relations, Pew Research Center, March 2, 2005, www.pewresearch.org/religion/2005/03/02/faith-and -conflict-the-global-rise-of-christianity/.

[3]Adapted from the prayer "For an Anniversary of One Departed," *Book of Common Prayer* (Huntington Beach, CA: Anglican Liturgy Press, 2019), 678.

9. AGNES TSAO KOU YING, LUCY YI ZHENMEI, AND AGATHA LIN ZHAO

[1]Paul Hattaway, *China's Book of Martyrs* (Carlisle, CA: Piquant Editions, 2007), 289.

[2]"Global Christianity—A Report on the Size and Distribution of the World's Christian Population," Pew Research Center, December 19, 2011, www.pewresearch.org/religion/2011/12/19 /global-christianity-exec/.

[3]Adapted from prayer "For the Coming of God's Kingdom," *Book of Common Prayer* (Huntington Beach, CA: Anglican Liturgy Press, 2019), 603.

10. POLYCARP

[1] Common paraphrase of the translation found in *The Martyrdom of Polycarp*, 9–10, 13–16, 18–19; see also *The Apostolic Fathers II*, ed. and trans. Bart D. Ehrman (Cambridge, MA: Harvard University Press, 2003), 307–46.

[2] *The Apostolic Fathers*, trans. Rick Brannan (Bellingham, WA: Lexham Press, 2017), 128.

[3] From the collect for "The Fourth Sunday of Epiphany," *Book of Common Prayer* (Huntington Beach, CA: Anglican Liturgy Press, 2019), 602.

11. PERPETUA AND FELICITY

[1] "Martyrdom of Perpetua and Felicity," trans. Herbert Musurillo, in *The Acts of the Christian Martyrs*, Henry Chadwick, ed. (Oxford: Oxford University Press, 1972), 111.

[2] "Martyrdom of Perpetua and Felicity," 111.

[3] "Martyrdom of Perpetua and Felicity," 111.

[4] "Martyrdom of Perpetua and Felicity," 125.

[5] "Martyrdom of Perpetua and Felicity," 119.

[6] Adapted from the commemoration "Of a Martyr," *Book of Common Prayer* (Huntington Beach, CA: Anglican Liturgy Press, 2019), 637.

12. HARRIET TUBMAN

[1] Angela Tate, "Harriet Tubman: Life, Liberty and Legacy," National Museum of African American History and Culture, https://nmaahc.si.edu/explore/stories/harriet-tubman.

[2] Tate, "Harriet Tubman."

[3] Sarah Bradford, *Scenes in the Life of Harriet Tubman* (Auburn, NY: W. J. Moses, Printer, 1869), https://docsouth.unc.edu/neh/bradford/bradford.html.

[4] Bradford, *Scenes in the Life of Harriet Tubman*, 20.

[5] Francis Schaeffer, *No Little People*, in *The Complete Works of Francis Schaeffer*, vol. 3 (Wheaton IL: Crossway, 1982).

[6] Adapted from the commemoration "Of a Renewer of Society," *Book of Common Prayer* (Huntington Beach, CA: Anglican Liturgy Press, 2019), 640.

13. PATRICK

[1] *Pocket Celtic Prayers*, comp. Martin Wallace (Cambridge: Church House Publishing, 2004), 30.

[2] Saint Patrick, *The Confession of Saint Patrick*, transl. Sean McGowan (Apollo, PA: Ichthus Publications, 2018).

[3] Saint Patrick, *The Confession of Saint Patrick*.

[4] *The Liturgy of the Hours, Lenten Season, Easter Season* (New York: Catholic Book Publishing, 1976).

[5] "Saint Patrick's Breastplate," hymn 333, attributed to Saint Patrick, translated by Cecil Frances Alexander, *The Book of Common Praise* (Huntington Beach, CA: Anglican Liturgy Press, 2017).

14. ÓSCAR ROMERO

[1] Óscar Romero, *The Violence of Love*, trans. James Brockman, SJ (New York: Harper & Row, 1988), 43.

[2] Giulia Galeotti, "Oscar Romero and the Poor," Eternal Word Television Network blog, www.ewtn.com/catholicism/library/oscar-romero-and-the-poor-5793.

[3] Filip Mazurkczak, "Archbishop Romero and Liberation Theology," National Catholic Register, May 7, 2015, www.ncregister.com/news/archbishop-romero-and-liberation-theology-acs6n5kf.

[4] Romero, *Violence of Love*, 54.

[5] "Archbishop Óscar Romero: The Last Sermon (1980)," Internet Archive, https://archive.org/details/the-last-sermon-of-archbishop-oscar-romero/mode/2up.

[6]"El Salvador: Something Vile in This Land," *Time*, April 14, 1980.

[7]Thomas Hobbes, *Leviathan* (Oxford: Oxford University Press, 2009).

[8]Frederick Christian Bauerschmidt, *The Love That Is God* (Grand Rapids, MI: Eerdmans, 2020), 78.

[9]Adapted from the prayer "For Social Justice," *Book of Common Prayer* (Huntington Beach, CA: Anglican Liturgy Press, 2019), 659.

15. MARY OF EGYPT

[1]Sophronios of Jerusalem, "Life of Saint Mary of Egypt" from *The Great Canon, the Work of Saint Andrew of Crete*, Holy Trinity Monastery, https://web.archive.org/web/20101230181728, http://monachos.net/content/patristics/patristictexts/182-life-of-mary.

[2]Sophronios of Jerusalem, "Life of Saint Mary of Egypt."

[3]Adapted from the prayer "In Times of Suffering & Weakness," *Book of Common Prayer* (Huntington Beach, CA. Anglican Liturgy Press, 2019), 674.

16. MARTIN LUTHER KING JR.

[1]Martin Luther King Jr., *Strength to Love* (Minneapolis: Fortress Press, 2010), 101.

[2]King, *Strength to Love*, 17.

[3]D. J. Marotta, *Liturgy in the Wilderness* (Chicago: Moody Publishers, 2022).

[4]Taylor Branch, *Parting the Waters: America in the King Years, 1954–1963* (New York: Simon & Schuster, 1998).

[5]Adapted from the "Thanksgiving for the Diversity of Races and Cultures," *Book of Common Prayer* (Huntington Beach, CA: Anglican Liturgy Press, 2019), 682.

17. DIETRICH BONHOEFFER

[1]Dietrich Bonhoeffer, *Letters and Papers from Prison* (New York: Macmillan, 1967), 73.

[2]Dietrich Bonhoeffer, *The Cost of Discipleship* (Nashville: Broadman & Holman, 1998), 11.

[3]"Dietrich Bonhoeffer: German Theologian and Resister," *Christianity Today*, www.christianitytoday.com/history/people/martyrs/dietrich-bonhoeffer.html.

[4]Dietrich Bonhoeffer, *Life Together* (New York: Harper & Brothers, 1954), 26–27.

[5]Bonhoeffer, *Life Together*, 28–29.

[6]Adapted from the prayer "For Trustfulness in Times of Worry and Anxiety," *Book of Common Prayer* (Huntington Beach, CA: Anglican Liturgy Press, 2019), 670.

18. KATERI TEKAKWITHA

[1]K. I. Koppedrayer, *The Making of the First Iroquois Virgin: Early Jesuit Biographies of the Blessed Kateri Tekakwitha* (Durham, NC: Duke University Press, 1993), 287.

[2]B. M. Kelly, "Blessed Kateri Tekakwitha" in *The Catholic Encyclopedia* (New York: Robert Appleton Company, 1912), accessed July 22, 2023, www.newadvent.org/cathen/14471a.htm.

[3]Adapted from the prayer for "Knowing and Loving God," *Book of Common Prayer* (Huntington Beach, CA: Anglican Liturgy Press, 2019), 668.

19. CATHERINE OF SIENA

[1]Kelly Marcum, "St. Catherine of Siena's Fire Was Stoked in Conversation with God," *National Catholic Register*, April 29, 2023, www.ncregister.com/blog/fire-of-st-catherine-of-siena.

[2]"Catherine of Siena, Letter 16, Dicastery for the Clergy," Clerus, www.clerus.org/bibliaclerusonline/it/eki.htm#q.

[3]Adapted from "Collect for A Holy Life," *The 1662 Book of Common Prayer* (Downers Grove, IL: InterVarsity Press, 2021), 668.

20. PANDITA MARY RAMABAI

[1]Surindur Kaur, "4 Incredible Christian Women Who Changed India," *Christianity Today*, March 8, 2023, www.christianitytoday.com/ct/2023/march-web-only/indian-christian-women-pandita-ramabai-cornelia-sorabji.html.

[2]"Overlooked No More: Pandita Ramabai, Indian Scholar, Feminist and Educator," *New York Times*, November 26, 2018.

[3]Keith J. White, "Jesus Was Her Guru," *Christianity Today*, 2005, www.christianitytoday.com /history/issues/issue-87/jesus-was-her-guru.html.

[4]Adapted from "Prayers for the Commemoration of a Saint," *The 1662 Book of Common Prayer* (Downers Grove, IL: InterVarsity Press, 2021), 712.

21. ATHANASIUS

[1]Athanasius of Alexandria, *Saint Athanasius of Alexandria Collection* (Hawthorne, CA: Aeterna Press, 2016), 312.

[2]Joseph Kohm Jr., "Athanasius: The Incarnation of the Word of God," C. S. Lewis Institute, winter 2007, www.cslewisinstitute.org/wp-content/uploads/KD-2017-Winter-Athanasius -The-Incarnation-of-the-Word-of-God-6208.pdf.

[3]Philip Schaff and Henry Wace, eds., *A Select Library of Nicene and Post-Nicene Fathers of the Christian Church*, vol. 7 (Peabody, MA: Hendrickson Publishers, 2012), 1,886–89.

[4]Adapted from the prayer for Trinity Sunday, *Book of Common Prayer* (Huntington Beach, CA: Anglican Liturgy Press, 2019), 615.

22. JULIAN OF NORWICH

[1]"For Satisfaction in Christ," *Book of Common Prayer* (Huntington Beach, CA: Anglican Liturgy Press, 2019), 673.

[2]Julian of Norwich, *Revelations of Divine Love* (New York: Penguin Books, 1966), 63.

[3]Norwich, *Revelations of Divine Love*, 68.

[4]Robert Farrar Capon, *The Supper of the Lamb* (New York: Random House, Inc, 1967), 5.

[5]Christopher Watkin, *Biblical Critical Theory* (Grand Rapids, MI: Zondervan, 2022), 59–60.

[6]"For Satisfaction in Christ," *Book of Common Prayer*, 673.

23. MARTYRS OF SUDAN

[1]*Holy Women, Holy Men* (New York: Church Publishing, 2011), 370.

[2]*Holy Women, Holy Men*, 370.

[3]"South Sudan 2022 International Religious Freedom Report," US State Department, www .state.gov/wp-content/uploads/2023/05/441219-SOUTH-SUDAN-2022-INTERNATIONAL -RELIGIOUS-FREEDOM-REPORT.pdf.

[4]Gabrielle Tétrault-Farber, "Sudan Could Soon Have 10 Million Internally Displaced People, UN Agency Says," Reuters, June 7, 2024, www.reuters.com/world/africa/sudan-could-soon -have-10-mln-internally-displaced-people-un-agency-says-2024-06-07/.

[5]Edmund P. Clowney, *Called to Ministry* (Phillipsburg, NJ: Presbyterian & Reformed Pub. Co., 1964).

[6]Adapted from the prayer "For the Persecuted Church," *The 1662 Book of Common Prayer* (Downers Grove, IL: InterVarsity Press, 2021), 678.

24. ALCUIN

[1]Jitney Nelson, "Alcuin's Letter to Meginfrid" in *Penser la paysannerie medievale, un defi impossible?*, Alain Dierkens, et al., eds. (Paris: Sorbonne University Press, 2017), https://books openedition.org/psorbonne/27986.

[2]Nelson, "Alcuin's Letter to Meginfird."

[3]Alcuin, "Letter 56 in Stephen Allott," *Alcuin of York* (York, England: The Ebor Press, 1974).

[4]John Dickson, *Bullies and Saints: An Honest Look at the Good and Evil of Christian History* (Grand Rapids, MI: Zondervan, 2021).

[5]J. R. R. Tolkien, *The Fellowship of the Ring* (Boston: Houghton Mifflin, 1982), 104.

[6]Adapted from the "Prayer for Schools, Colleges, and Universities," *Book of Common Prayer* (Huntington Beach, CA: Anglican Liturgy Press, 2019), 661.

25. JOAN OF ARC

[1]"St. Joan of Arc," The Roman Catholic Diocese of Baton Rouge, May 17, 2022, www.diobr
.org/news/st-joan-of-arc.

[2]Lacey Baldwin Smith, *Fools, Martyrs, Traitors: The Story of Martyrdom in the Western World* (New York: Alfred A. Knopf, 1997), 11.

[3]Adapted from the prayer "In a Time of War," *The 1662 Book of Common Prayer* (Downers Grove, IL: InterVarsity Press, 2021), 672.

26. JUSTIN

[1]Justin Martyr, "First Apology," *Ante-Nicene Fathers*, vol. 1, fifth edition (Peabody, MA: Hendrickson Publishers, 2012), 167.

[2]Martyr, "First Apology," 167.

[3]Martyr, "First Apology," 186.

[4]Adapted from "Prayers for the Commemoration of a Saint," *The 1662 Book of Common Prayer* (Downers Grove, IL: InterVarsity Press, 2021), 712.

27. SUNDAR SINGH

[1]Sundar Singh, *Wisdom of the Sadhu Teachings of Sundar Singh* (Walden, NY: Plough Publishing, 2014), 152.

[2]Singh, *Wisdom of the Sadhu Teachings*, 176.

[3]Singh, *Wisdom of the Sadhu Teachings*, 43.

[4]Singh, *Wisdom of the Sadhu Teachings*, 15.

[5]Sadhu Sundar Singh, *Meditations on Various Aspects of the Spiritual Life* (London: Macmillan and Co., Limited, 1926), 30.

[6]Adapted from the "Prayer for the Commemoration of a Missionary or Evangelist," *Book of Common Prayer* (Huntington Beach, CA: Anglican Liturgy Press, 2019), 638.

28. MOSES THE ETHIOPIAN

[1]"Divine Humility," Saint Gregory the Illuminator Armenian Church (June 6, 2022), https://stgregorychicago.org/2022/06/16/divine-humility/.

[2]"History of St. Moses the Black Priory," St. Moses the Black Priory, https://web.archive.org/web/20110829205900, http://stmosestheblackpriory.org/about_history.html.

[3]*Give Me a Word: The Alphabetical Sayings of the Desert Fathers*, trans. John Wortley (Yonkers, NY: St. Vladimir's Seminary Press, 2014), 198.

[4]*Give Me a Word*, 198.

[5]Adapted from the "Prayer for the Commemoration of a Monastic or Religious," *Book of Common Prayer* (Huntington Beach, CA: Anglican Liturgy Press, 2019), 639.

29. BENEDICT AND SCHOLASTICA

[1]Saint Benedict, *Rule of Saint Benedict: A Commentary by the Right Rev. Dom Paul Delatte* (London: Burns & Oats & Washbourne, 1921), 5.

[2]Saint Gregory the Great, *Dialogues*, bk. 2, trans. Myra L. Uhlfedler (New York: The Bobbs-Merrill Company, Inc., 1967), 43.

[3]Saint Gregory the Great, *Dialogues*, bk. 2, ch. 4.

[4]*Early Christian Lives*, trans. Carolinne White (London: Penguin Books, 1998), 198–99.

[5]Benedict, *Rule of Saint Benedict*, ch. 53.

[6]"For Grace to Seek God in Every Way," *Book of Common Prayer* (Huntington Beach, CA: Anglican Liturgy Press, 2019), 672.

30. OLGA AND VLADIMIR

[1]Samuel Hazzard Cross and Olgerd P. Sherbowitz-Wetzor, trans. and eds., *The Russian Primary Chronicle: Laurentian Text* (Cambridge, MA: The Medieval Academy of America, 1953), 82.

[2]Hazzard Cross and Sherbowitz-Wetzor, *Russian Primary Chronicle*, 82.

[3]Hazzard Cross and Sherbowitz-Wetzor, *Russian Primary Chronicle*, 82.
[4]Serge A. Zenkovsky, ed., *Medieval Russia's Epics, Chronicles, and Tales* (New York: E.P. Dutton & Co, 1963).
[5]Adapted from the prayer "Of Any Commemoration," *Book of Common Prayer* (Huntington Beach, CA: Anglican Liturgy Press, 2019), 640.

31. MACRINA
[1]Bert Ghezzi, *Voices of the Saints: 365-Day Journey with our Spiritual Companions* (Chicago: Loyola Press, 2009).
[2]Gregory of Nyssa, *The Life of Macrina*, https://tertullian.org/fathers/gregory_macrina_1_life.htm.
[3]Adapted from "Prayers for the Commemoration of a Saint," *The 1662 Book of Common Prayer* (Downers Grove, IL: InterVarsity Press, 2021), 712.

32. MARGARET OF ANTIOCH
[1]*St. Marina (Margaret), Great Martyr, of Antioch in Pisidia*, Antiochian Orthodox Christian Archdiocese, http://ww1.antiochian.org/node/19000.
[2]Adapted from the prayer "For Proper 26," *Book of Common Prayer* (Huntington Beach, CA: Anglican Liturgy Press, 2019), 622.

33. JOHANN SEBASTIAN BACH
[1]Gregory Bateson, "Form, Substance and Difference," *ETC: A Review of General Semantics* 72, no. 1 (2015): 90–104, www.jstor.org/stable/24761998, accessed October 11, 2023.
[2]Lewis Thomas, *The Lives of a Cell: Notes of a Biology Watcher* (New York: Viking Press, 1974), 53.
[3]Patrick Kavanaugh, *Spiritual Lives of the Great Composers* (Grand Rapids, MI: Zondervan, 1996), 20.
[4]John F. Goodman, *Mingus Speaks* (Oakland, CA: University of California Press, 2003), 25.
[5]Kavanaugh, *Spiritual Lives of the Great Composers*, 23.
[6]Kavanaugh, *Spiritual Lives of the Great Composers*, 20.
[7]"110 Alain de Botton Quotes on Marriage, Success, and Work," Quotlr, https://quotlr.com/author/alain-de-botton.
[8]Adapted from the prayer "For Church Musicians and Artists," *Book of Common Prayer* (Huntington Beach, CA: Anglican Liturgy Press, 2019), 650.

34. OLAUDAH EQUIANO AND WILLIAM WILBERFORCE
[1]Olaudah Equiano, or Gustavus Vassa, *The Interesting Narrative of the Life of Olaudah Equiano, or Gustavus Vassa, the African. Written by Himself* (London: Author, 1789), vol. 1, 70–88.
[2]William Hague, *William Wilberforce: The Life of the Great Anti-Slave Trade Campaigner* (New York: Harcourt, Inc., 2007), 232.
[3]"William Wilberforce: Antislavery Politician," *Christianity Today*, www.christianitytoday.com/history/people/activists/william-wilberforce.html.
[4]Frederick Buechner, *Wishful Thinking* (San Francisco: Harper One, 1993), 118–19.
[5]Adapted from "A Prayer of Self-Dedication (by William Temple)," *Book of Common Prayer* (Huntington Beach, CA: Anglican Liturgy Press, 2019), 668.

35. AUGUSTINE AND MONICA
[1]Augustine, *Confessions*, trans. Henry Chadwick (New York: Oxford University Press, 1998).
[2]Augustine, *Confessions*.
[3]Augustine, *Confessions*.
[4]Augustine, *Confessions*.
[5]Adapted from the prayer for "The Third Sunday of Lent," *Book of Common Prayer* (Huntington Beach, CA: Anglican Liturgy Press, 2019), 606.

36. JOHN BUNYAN

[1]John Bunyan, *The Pilgrim's Progress* (New York: Barnes & Noble Classics, 2005), 226.
[2]John Bunyan, *Grace Abounding to the Chief of Sinners* (Nashville: Word Publishing, 1991), 21.
[3]Bunyan, *Grace Abounding to the Chief of Sinners*, 90–91.
[4]*The Cambridge History of English and American Literature in 18 Volumes (1907–21),* Volume VII.
[5]J. Chapman, *The Westminster Review* 138 (1892): 610.
[6]John Bunyan, *John Bunyan: Legacy of Faith Library* (Nashville: B&H Publishing Group, 2017), 155.
[7]C. S. Lewis, *The Last Battle* (New York: Harper Collins, 2008), 196.
[8]Adapted from the prayer for "The Sixth Sunday of Easter (Rogation)," *Book of Common Prayer* (Huntington Beach, CA: Anglican Liturgy Press, 2019), 613.

37. LUCIAN TAPIEDI

[1]Robert Atwell and Christopher L. Webber, eds., *Celebrating the Saints: Devotional Readings for Saint's Days* (Harrisburg, PA: Morehouse Publishing, 2001), 290.
[2]Philip Strong, "Message to Mission Staff," radio broadcast, January 31, 1942, http://anglicanhistory .org/aus/png/strong_message1942.html.
[3]Atwell and Webber, *Celebrating the Saints*, 290.
[4]Alan Briggs, *Stay Forth* (Colorado Springs, CO: NavPress, 2015), 149.
[5]Adapted from the prayer for "The Communion of Saints" *Book of Common Prayer* (Huntington Beach, CA: Anglican Liturgy Press, 2019), 679.

38. TERESA OF CALCUTTA ("MOTHER TERESA")

[1]Mother Teresa, *Do Something Beautiful for God: The Essential Teachings of Mother Teresa* (North Palm Beach, FL: Blue Sparrow, 2019).
[2]Louise Chipley Slavicek, *Mother Teresa: Caring for the World's Poor* (New York: Chelsea House, 2007), 90.
[3]Adapted from the prayer "For Those Who Serve Others," *Book of Common Prayer* (Huntington Beach, CA: Anglican Liturgy Press, 2019), 660.

39. HILDEGARD

[1]Hildegard von Bingen, "All of Creation Is a Song of Praise," www.musicanet.org/textes /02/81129.htm.
[2]Joe Staines, *The Rough Guide to Classical Music* (London: Rough Guides LTD, 2010), 256.
[3]"The Life and Works of Hildegard von Bingen (1098-1179)," Kenyon College, www2.kenyon .edu/projects/margin/hildegar.htm, accessed June 12, 2024.
[4]Adapted from the prayer "For Right Use of This World's Goods," *The 1662 Book of Common Prayer* (Downers Grove, IL: InterVarsity Press, 2021), 694.

40. ANDREW KIM TAEGON

[1]*From the Final Exhortation of Andrew Kim Taegon, Priest and Martyr,* Liturgy of the Hours © 1973, 1974, 1975, ICEL, www.liturgies.net/saints/andrewkimtaegon/readings.htm#loh.
[2]*Butler's Lives of the Saints: New Concise Edition* (London: Burns & Oats, 1985).
[3]*Final Exhortation of Andrew Kim Taegon.*
[4]C. S. Lewis, *The Voyage of the Dawn Treader* (New York: MacMillan, 1952), 159–60.
[5]Adapted from the prayer for "Proper 16," *Book of Common Prayer* (Huntington Beach, CA: Anglican Liturgy Press, 2019), 619.

41. FRANCIS OF ASSISI

[1]Francis of Asissi, *The Writings of St. Francis of Assisi*, trans. Paschal Robinson, part I, admonition #27 (Philadelphia: The Dolphin Press, 1906), 19.
[2]Leopold de Cherance, *Saint Francis of Asissi* (London: Burns & Oats, 1900), 27.

[3]"For Participation in the Peace of God," *Book of Common Prayer* (Huntington Beach, CA: Anglican Liturgy Press, 2019), 672.

42. WILLIAM TYNDALE

[1]William Tyndale, *The Obedience of a Christian Man* (New York: Penguin, 2000).

[2]John Foxe, *The Acts and Monuments of John Foxe*, vol. 5 (Charleston, SC: BiblioBazaar, 2009), 127.

[3]Adapted from the commemoration "Of a Pastor," *Book of Common Prayer* (Huntington Beach, CA: Anglican Liturgy Press, 2019), 638.

43. ESTHER JOHN

[1]"Esther John," Westminster Abbey, www.westminster-abbey.org/abbey-commemorations /commemorations/esther-john.

[2]Adapted from the prayer "For Missionary Societies," *Book of Common Prayer* (Huntington Beach, CA: Anglican Liturgy Press, 2019), 651.

44. TERESA OF ÁVILA

[1]Teresa of Ávila, "Poem IX" in *Complete Works St. Teresa of Ávila*, E. Allison Peers, ed., vol. 3 (New York: Sheed & Ward, 1946), 288.

[2]*The Sixteenth Century in 100 Women* (n.p.: Pen & Sword History, 2023), 208.

[3]Adapted from the commemoration "Of a Reformer of the Church," *Book of Common Prayer* (Huntington Beach, CA: Anglican Liturgy Press, 2019), 639.

45. MARTIN OF PORRES

[1]Mary Fabyan Windeatt, *St. Martin De Porres: The Story of the Little Doctor of Lima, Peru* (Rockford, IL: Tan Books, 1993).

[2]Adapted from the prayer "For the Medical Professions," *Book of Common Prayer* (Huntington Beach, CA: Anglican Liturgy Press, 2019), 661.

46. HERMAN OF ALASKA

[1]Saint Herman of Alaska Brotherhood, *Saint Herman of Alaska: His Life and Service* (Plantina, CA: Saint Herman of Alaska Brotherhood, 2007), 15.

[2]Adapted from the prayer "For the Mission of the Church," *Book of Common Prayer* (Huntington Beach, CA: Anglican Liturgy Press, 2019), 650.

47. HILDA OF WHITBY

[1]Bede, *Ecclesiastical History of the English People*, trans. Leo Sherley-Price (London: Penguin Classics, Revised Edition, 1990), 246.

[2]Bede, *Ecclesiastical History*, 246.

[3]Adapted from the prayer "For Holy Thought," *Book of Common Prayer* (Huntington Beach, CA: Anglican Liturgy Press, 2019), 668.

48. CLIVE STAPLES LEWIS

[1]C. S. Lewis, *The Weight of Glory* (San Francisco: Harper Collins, 2001), 46.

[2]C. S. Lewis, *Surprised by Joy* (New York: Harcourt, 1955), 115.

[3]C. S. Lewis, *A Grief Observed* (San Francisco: Harper Collins, 1996), 66.

[4]Lewis, *Grief Observed*, 65.

[5]Lewis, *Weight of Glory*, 46.

[6]Adapted from the prayer "For an Ecumenist," *Book of Common Prayer* (Huntington Beach, CA: Anglican Liturgy Press, 2019), 639.

49. JOHN OF DAMASCUS

[1]John of Damascus, *First Apology for Against Those Who Attack the Divine Images*, trans. David Anderson (Crestwood, NY: St. Vladimir's Seminary Press, 1980).

[2]Adapted from "For Joy in God's Creation," *The 1662 Book of Common Prayer* (Downers Grove, IL: InterVarsity Press, 2021), 670.

50. NICHOLAS ("SANTA CLAUS")

[1]Greek Orthodox Archdiocese of Australia, www.stparaskevi.org.au/the-giver-of-every-good -and-perfect-gift-has-called-upon-us-to-mimic-his-giving-by-grace-through-faith-and-this -is-not-of-ourselves-2/.

[2]Craig Blomberg, *Christians in an Age of Wealth* (Grand Rapids, MI: Zondervan, 2013), 243.

[3]Adapted from the prayer "For Stewardship of Creation," *Book of Common Prayer* (Huntington Beach, CA: Anglican Liturgy Press, 2019), 652.

51. LUCY

[1]"December 13, St. Lucy, V.M." in *Anglican Breviary* (New York: The Frank Gavin Liturgical Foundation, Inc., 1998), E35.

[2]Adapted from the collect for "The First Sunday in Advent," *Book of Common Prayer* (Huntington Beach, CA: Anglican Liturgy Press, 2019), 598.

52. NINO OF GEORGIA

[1]"Saint Nino (Nina), Equal of the Apostles, Enlightener of Georgia," Orthodox Church in America, www.oca.org/saints/lives/2013/01/14/100191-saint-nino-nina-equal-of-the-apostles -enlightener-of-georgia.

[2]"Saint Nino," Orthodox Church in America.

[3]"Saint Nino," Orthodox Church in America.

[4]Adapted from "Prayers for the Commemoration of a Saint," *The 1662 Book of Common Prayer* (Downers Grove, IL: InterVarsity Press, 2021), 712.

APPENDIX A: CHURCH HISTORY SURVEY

[1]A popular adaptation of the words of the second/third century Christian author Tertullian in his Apology, "the blood of Christians is seed" (Sydney Thelwall translation).

[2]"Global Christianity—A Report on the Size & Distribution of the World's Christian Population," Pew Research Center, www.pewresearch.org/religion/2011/12/19/global-christianity -exec/.

[3]"The Future of World Religions: Population Growth Projections," Pew Research Center, www .pewresearch.org/religion/2015/04/02/christians/#:~:text=The%20world%27s%20Christian %20population%20is,to%202.9%20billion%20in%202050.&text=Nearly%20one%2Din% Dthree%20people,same%20share%20as%20in%202010.

[4]"Global Christianity," Pew Research Center.

[5]"North to South: A Reappraisal of Anglican Communion Membership Figures," *Journal of Anglican Studies*, October 2015, Cambridge University.

[6]"Global Catholic Population," Pew Research Center, www.pewresearch.org/religion /2013/02/13/the-global-catholic-population/.

[7]"Christianity in China," Council on Foreign Relations, www.cfr.org/backgrounder/christianity -china.

[8]Gina A. Zurlo, Todd M. Johnson, and Peter F. Crossing, "World Christianity 2024: Fragmentation and Unity," *International Bulletin of Mission Research*, vol. 48(1):12, January 1, 2024.

Like this book?
Scan the code to discover more content like this!

Get on IVP's email list to receive special offers, exclusive book news, and thoughtful content from your favorite authors on topics you care about.